What the critics said about *It Takes Two To Toyi-Toyi*:

"... he has achieved that most difficult of satirical undertakings: he has written what is at once a very funny and very serious book." Robert Kirby, *Sunday Times*

"... Mr Silber has come of age as a humorist ... The book is a comic glory." Will Bernard, *Talking of Books,* Radio South Africa

"In this irreverent, sobering and hilarious survival guide, Gus shoots straight from the hip with devilish delight, and the result is a satirical masterpiece." *Woman Wise*

"I admire the man's ability to shake the sacred cows ... Politicians across the board should be force-fed daily excerpts from this book ..." Martin McGhee, *The Citizen*

"You'll recognise yourselves in the pages of this book. It's side-splitting, finger-wagging fun — just the kind of medicine seriously sullen South Africans need." J Bennett, *Sunday Tribune*

"... hilarious rollicking *knowledgeable* fun." *Living*

"This humorous look at the trials and tribulations of a country in the midst of horror and change provides light relief at a time it is needed most." *Woman's Value*

"Much of the humour derives from unexpected twists after beguilingly accurate, deadpan descriptions of things typical in the 'New South Africa'." Martin Williams, *Natal Witness*

"There are no sacred cows ... his rapier-like wit attacks everything from the ANC switchboard to SABC hairdos ... Silber makes us laugh at ourselves." Ashley Hayden, *Sunday Times*

"Carry on with Gus-to. If only because it makes us laugh at our own lunacy, *It Takes Two To Toyi-Toyi* takes my vote for the New South African Book of the Year." *The Indicator*

# Braaivleis of the Vanities

*How to stay sane in South Africa*

# Gus Silber

**with illustrations by Anthony Stidolph**

PENGUIN BOOKS

PENGUIN BOOKS

Published by the Penguin Group
27 Wrights Lane, London W8 5TZ
Viking Penguin, a division of Penguin Books USA Inc, 375 Hudson Street, New York, New York 10014, USA
Penguin Books Australia Ltd, Ringwood, Victoria, Australia
Penguin Books Canada Ltd, 10 Alcorn Avenue, Toronto, Ontario, Canada M4V 3B2
Penguin Books (NZ) Ltd, 182-190 Wairau Road, Auckland 10, New Zealand
Penguin Books, Amethyst Street, Theta Ext 1, Johannesburg, South Africa

Penguin Books Ltd, Registered Offices: Harmondsworth, Middlesex, England

First published by Penguin Books 1992

Copyright © Text Gus Silber 1992
          © Illustrations Anthony Stidolph 1992

All rights reserved

The moral right of the author has been asserted.

ISBN 0 140 17766 3

Typeset by GraphicSet
Printed and bound by Creda Press
Cover designed by Hadaway Illustration & Design

Except in the United States of America, this book is sold subject to the condition that it shall not, by way of trade or otherwise, be lent, resold, hired out, or otherwise circulated without the publisher's prior consent in any form of binding or cover other than that in which it is published and without a similar condition including this condition being imposed on the subsequent purchaser.

# *Foreword Of The Vanities*

I have been asked to write the foreword to this comprehensive and practical guidebook on How to Stay Sane in South Africa today. It gives me great pleasure to accept this invitation, even though I was not on the author's original shortlist of 'The Top 50 People I Would Like to Get to Write the Foreword, If Only to Save Myself the Trouble of Having to Do It'.

The author told me his original intention was to persuade 'someone in high office' to write the foreword, but the lifts were out of order due to mass action by the Lift and Allied Workers' Union of South Africa (LAWUSA), and he did not feel like climbing 42 flights of stairs to the office in question.

I have therefore stepped in at the last minute to write this foreword, but before I begin, I would like to say a few words about the whole business of writing forewords.

First of all, a recent survey of 64 people (seated) and 22 people (standing) who were reading a book while travelling to work in a bus, revealed that seven out of ten people do not read forewords, while two out of ten people only read forewords because they are getting off at the next stop. The tenth respondent was unable to answer because he was driving the bus.

Despite these statistics, very few books are written without forewords, and many authors admit that they look forward to writing the foreword more than almost any other part of the book.

The reason for this is that forewords are generally written afterwards, and they therefore provide authors with a convenient excuse for telling the publishers that 'The book is just about finished. All I really have to do is find someone to do the foreword. Just give me a few more weeks. Thanks, the Author.'

One exception to this rule is *The Penguin Book of Forewords,* a book consisting entirely of forewords that were delivered to the publishers so long after the rest of the book, that no one could remember what they had done with the original manuscript. This riveting compilation is highly recommended for all foreword-thinking persons who have to get off at the next stop.

Right. Now for the foreword. 'Fore'. Having got that out of the way, all that really needs to be said is that I hereby declare this book well and truly open, and I hope that you get as much comprehensive and practical use out of it, as I hope to get a reasonable fee for having written this foreword.

Thank you.

The Author
Johannesburg
South Africa
Monday, Mass Action Day, 1992

# *All Stressed Up And No Place To Go*
## *A practical guide to staying safe and sane in South Africa today*

According to a recent survey specially commissioned for this sentence, nine out of ten South Africans are 'very optimistic' about the future of the country to which they are emigrating.

A further 17 out of 20 said they were adopting a 'wait and see' attitude on the question of whether their emigration visa applications would be approved, while a staggering 92 per cent of people coming out of the pub described themselves as 'confused and uncertain', having forgotten the question they had just been asked.

As these statistics clearly indicate, South Africans of virtually all creeds, cultures, and political perspectives are today caught in the grip of one of the most profound crises of confidence in the country's history.

'I am afraid to say that I have lost all confidence in the history of this country,' said a Professor Emeritus of South African History as he prepared to board his one-way flight to the tropical paradise island of Pago Pago, now open to all South African passport-holders who voted 'Yes' in the Referendum.

And yet, despite the allure of a new life and a brighter future in a land with a stable social and political climate, many South Africans are beginning to realise that the grass is not always greener on the other side of the security fence.

'For a dazzling green expanse of Kikuyu or Cape Buffalo, ask your gardener to water the lawn twice a day, and feed with generous amounts of limestone ammonium nitrate every four to six weeks,' advises Keith Kirstenbosch, one of South Africa's foremost experts in the field of grass.

'If this does not work, try spraying your lawn with fixed copper fungicide or a can of "Emerald Green" spray-paint manufactured in Australia. I'll send you some by airmail as soon as I get there.'

But for those South Africans who have made a firm decision to stick to their roots, South Africa remains a land of almost limitless opportunity, with sunny blue skies, wide horizons, and clouds of black smoke billowing through suburban backyards on a lazy Sunday afternoon.

This is easily avoided, however, by sprinkling a layer of slightly damp hickory wood-chips over the week's newspapers before setting fire to your braai. Make sure you take a good look through the classified supplements first, as there are some good bargains to be found under 'Emigrants' Excess Baggage For Sale'.

'Staying put in South Africa definitely has its advantages,' argues one South African who is definitely committed to staying put. 'Just the other day, I managed to pick up a complete infra-red home security system, plus a hi-fi, video recorder, and leather motorcycle jacket, for an absolute steal. As a result, I am thinking about staying in South Africa even after I have completed my sentence.'

But whatever your personal political convictions, there can be little doubt that staying in South Africa today is a process fraught with stress, tension, frustration, and pent-up fury, as anyone who has ever attempted to query their telephone account will be quick to confirm.

'It is essential for South Africans caught up in the chaos and turmoil of the transitional process to take a long view of the social, political, and economic situation,' advises a top

South African clinical psychologist in a reverse-charges telephone call from Toronto.

For further information, please look under 'All Stressed Up and No Place to Go' in the Professional Advice section of your 087 telephone directory. There are 7 500 lines linked to a central computer with a soothing nasal monotone, so please keep trying if they are all engaged.

In the interim, we have asked some of South Africa's top decision-makers for their personal tips on combating stress in the current social, political, and economic climate.

'I am in receipt of your faxed request for a personal tip on combating stress in the current social, political, and economic climate,' said one top decision-maker from his office on the top floor of a big glass building in the central business district of Johannesburg.

'Unfortunately, I am not able to reply at the moment, as I have just hurled my facsimile machine out of the window.'

At a power breakfast on the other side of town, a top corporate decision-maker revealed that he could not decide whether to have marmalade or strawberry jam with his white or wholewheat toast. However, he denied allegations that he was suffering from stress induced by the current social, political, and economic climate.

'I am very happy to be in South Africa at this point in time,' he said, spreading marmalade and strawberry jam on his tie, 'as I have just been offered a job in Australia.'

According to a respondent from Pretoria, who may not be named because he is a Foreign Affairs Minister with a major South African Government organisation, one of the best methods of combating stress is to construct scale-model jet aeroplanes out of paper.

Here is his top-secret, step-by-step guide, hand-delivered by airmail just a few minutes ago:

1. Take one large piece of foolscap paper, such as this memorandum from the African National Congress.
2. Quickly read contents.
3. Hold right palm just above piece of paper.
4. Make fist.
5. Unclench fist after five minutes of steady, controlled breathing.
6. Carefully uncrumple large piece of paper, smoothing out creases and patching torn bits with sellotape.
7. Take hold of top left corner of paper, align with far right edge, and fold along resulting diagonal with thumbnail.
8. Open paper and repeat above step with top right corner.
9. Tell secretary you can't speak to the State President right now, but will phone back as soon as you are free.
10. Finish making jet-fighter plane. Add wing-flaps, Air Force markings, paper-clip in nose assembly, and two 20mm cannons (use matchsticks).
11. Stand on desk.
12. Hold plane between thumb and forefinger of right hand, and launch towards door as United Nations Special Envoy walks in for 11 o'clock appointment.
13. Return State President's telephone call, and draft reply to African National Congress after retrieving memorandum from bridge of United Nations Special Envoy's spectacles.

This method of combating stress has been officially ratified by Codesa's Non-Working Group 5, which has been assigned to find constructive things for delegates to do until negotiations get back in the air.

*Staying sane in South Africa: how to keep constitutional negotiations up in the air.*

Despite the obstacles, barriers, and hurdles that have yet to be overcome, many political figures approached for comment stressed that they were feeling 'more confident with every passing day' about their chances of becoming President.

One top political figure, who asked not to be named in case he fell off his horse, said his second-favourite method of combating stress was 'horse-riding'.

Asked what his favourite method was, he replied: 'I have always found that the single most effective method of combating stress is to declare war on people. So far this year, I have issued declarations of war to most of the major players on the South African political scene. Unfortunately, they were all too busy fighting to accept my invitation.'

If you are not a major player on the South African political scene, here are some expert tips and guidelines guaranteed to help you combat stress in the current social, political, and economic climate.

*1. DO NOT ENGAGE IN ANY CONVERSATIONS OF A POLITICAL NATURE.* According to research conducted by a leading South African Stress Analysis Institute, talking about politics is one of the top three causes of stress in South Africa today.

The other two are 'Trying to Get Through to Directory Enquiries', and 'Trying to Find an Empty Parking Bay Outside the Australian Embassy in Pretoria'.

While these two activities can be curtailed to some extent by a) not paying your telephone bill, and b) catching a minibus taxi to the Australian Embassy in Pretoria, you will need to exercise greater effort and concentration in order to avoid getting caught up in a stress-inducing conversation on South African politics.

You are therefore advised to steer well clear of any formal or informal discussion that appears to be heading in the direction of one or more of the following subjects: stress; mass action; the state of the nation; the state of one's destination; the state of the roads; the state of South African television; the weather; the weather in Toronto; sex; shopping; minibus taxis; the influence of pre-Raphaelite painting on Elizabethan ballad poetry; the influence of chutney marinade on precooked boerewors; Jani Allan; the Rand-Dollar Exchange rate; the Olympics; javelins; assegais; rugby; the All-Blacks; peace; democracy; politics; panic buttons; and the fact that you can't have a conversation about anything these days without getting into a raving political argument.

*2. GO OUT AND SEE A GOOD ARNOLD SCHWARZE-NEGGER MOVIE.* There's nothing like going out and seeing a good Arnold Schwarzenegger movie for taking your mind off violence, mayhem, mindless brutality, mass action, granite-jawed intransigence and malicious damage to property.

If there isn't a good Arnold Schwarzenegger movie showing at a theatre near you, stay home and watch the News on television.

*3. READ AN UPLIFTING BOOK.* Books on How to Lift Up Heavy Objects, such as book-cases, potjiekos pots, packing crates, and Volume One of *The Collected Letters to the Editor* of Mangosuthu Gatsha Buthelezi, are available from the Do-it-Yourself section of your local library.

*4. TAKE THE DOG FOR A WALK AROUND THE BLOCK.* According to a study by the Canine Obedience

Institute For a Democratic South Africa, taking the dog for a walk around the block can be one of the most effective methods of relieving any stress and tension that may be felt by the dog as a result of being cooped up inside all day with no one interesting to bite.

It is not necessary to plan your route beforehand, as the dog will usually know the way. However, the following commands are suggested for a relatively stress-free dog-walking experience: 'Heel', 'Sit', 'Stay', 'Behave', 'Stop Pulling', 'Slow Down', 'Leave Postman', 'Ignore Cat', 'Come Back', 'Here Boy', 'Let Go', and 'Help'.

*5. HAVE ANOTHER PIECE OF CHOCOLATE.*
Chocolate-eaters of all shades, from Albany to Dairy Milk to Mint Crunch to Fruit & Nut, know that every bar of chocolate contains a special emulsifying ingredient designed to relieve stress and encourage you to eat another piece of chocolate.

'Emulsifier E322' is what it says here on the contents list on the back of the wrapper, right next to 'Cocoa Butter', '1,5 Glasses of Milk (approx)', and 'Haven't You Got Anything Better to Do than Read the Contents List on the Back of a Chocolate Wrapper'.

Chocolate, a health-giving energy snack, is the favourite food of mountaineers, astronauts, soldiers on secret missions behind enemy lines, and people with nothing better to do than read the contents list on the back of a chocolate wrapper.

Available from your nearest emergency snack outlet in packs of more than one, chocolate is guaranteed to take a load off your mind and put it on your hips.

## 6. UPGRADE YOUR HOME SECURITY SYSTEM.

'Whenever I feel troubled by political scenarios, concerned about constitutional negotiations, or alarmed about a two percentage point drop in the BA Rate,' confesses one of South Africa's top unemployed constitutional negotiators, 'I always find it very relaxing to upgrade my home security system. So far this year, I have only had to do this 42 times.'

Thanks to political reforms and advances in home security technology, South Africa is now acknowledged as a world leader in this field, with South African firms supplying systems to several countries that did much better than us at the Olympics.

If you believe that security begins at home, here is a brief guide to some recent innovations designed to prepare you for the transition to a peaceful and democratic South Africa.

*The Neighbourhood Watchman.* This full-colour, multi-channel closed-circuit in-house video monitor system comes complete with stereo sound, fisheye and zoom lenses, swivel-mounted video-cameras, and professional-quality mixing-desk for instant slow-motion action replay.

While the Neighbourhood Watchman is unlikely to prevent people wearing full-face balaclavas from breaking into your property and liberating your possessions, it could come in very handy if you are ever called on to give evidence in a defamation action involving a former room-mate.

*The False Alarm System.* It looks like a real alarm, protects like a real alarm, and makes a noise like a real alarm, but don't worry — it's only a false alarm.

Primed to emit an ear-piercing signal the moment your cat climbs through the burglar bars or you press your panic button by mistake while trying to locate your house-keys at two o'clock in the morning, the false alarm system can be linked by radio to the control room of your neighbourhood security company.

For a nominal monthly fee, they will agree not to dispatch any uniformed personnel armed with bazookas and pump-action shotguns to the scene within seconds. This will save you the embarrassment of having to tell them it was only a false alarm, but thanks for coming anyway.

It is recommended that you supplement your false alarm system with a genuine alarm system, in case someone tries to break in and steal your cat.

*The Credit Card, the Half-Brick, and the Long Piece of Wire.* These items should be carried on your person at all times, in the event that you inadvertently lock yourself out of your house on your way to a pre-breakfast session with your stress-reduction therapist one Monday morning.

In order to retrieve your house and car keys from the fruit bowl on the kitchen table, or the inside pocket of the jacket you decided not to wear at the last minute because it had a dog-print on one of the cuffs, you will be forced to gain entry to your property by means of 'breaking and entering'.

Do not be alarmed. Since no one has yet managed to design a home security system that is completely foolproof, you should be able to do this even if it makes you feel like a complete fool.

First, use the half-brick to create an opening in a small window-pane convenient to the suspected location of your keys. Now hook the long piece of wire around the window-handle.

Through careful, patient manipulation, you should be able to force the window open from the inside. Although this will not help you to gain entry, it will at least allow some fresh air to filter into your house through the security bars.

Now try the credit card.

Anyone who has ever seen an American detective movie will know that it is possible to open a securely locked door by manoeuvring a credit card between the doorframe and the latch bolt assembly, providing you are an actor in an American detective movie. If not, don't worry.

A representative from your neighbourhood security company will be on the scene within minutes, and you will probably be let out on bail in time to telephone your insurance broker, your lawyer, and an after-hours locksmith.

*The 087 911 Number.* Inspired by the success of 087 lines and the *Rescue 911* television series, the 087 911 line is open 24 hours a day for instant response in case of emergency.

Please dial 087 911, followed by the two digits of your choice from the following handy table:

Help, I Feel Overcome By a Sudden Compulsion to Dial the First 087 Number I Come Across ..... 11
Help, the State President has Just Declared a State of Emergency .......................... 22
Help, I've Just Broken Into Somebody's House and There's Nothing Left to Steal Because Someone Else Got Here Before Me ........................ 33
Help, There's Nothing to Watch on TV Except *Rescue 911* ................................. 44
Help, I Can't Find a Single Thing to Wear ..... 55
Help, There's Someone Knocking at My Door .. 66
Don't Worry, it's Only the Postman With My Australian Emigration Visa ................... 77

*7. TAKE THE LONG VIEW.* According to a long-term projection by one of South Africa's most eminent scenario planners, the economic upswing is just around the corner from the second four-way stop-street after the roundabout.

Meanwhile, a negotiated solution to the constitutional impasse is straight ahead, over the koppie, into the donga, across the veld, on to the slip-road, left at the fork, right at the crossroads, through the toll-booth, straight across the speed-bumps at 140 kilometres per hour, and all the way around the detour until the next impasse.

Now all we need to do is find a driver for the minibus. Any volunteers?

# *Roll On Peace And Democracy*
## *How to participate in a rolling mass action campaign*

Monday, Mass Action Day, 1992, dawned like any other Monday, Mass Action Day in the history of South Africa. As the winter sun cast a bleary eye over the horizon, thousands of ordinary, everyday South Africans were rousing themselves from slumber for the ordinary working day that lay ahead.

Despite widespread calls for a stayaway and general strike by the ANC-COSATU-SACP alliance, throngs of eager workers were already thronging their way into bustling city centres, ready to occupy factories and offices for what was certain to be just another normal working day.

Many of these workers appeared to be so happy to be going to work, that they could hardly stop singing, dancing, chanting, and leaping into the air with excitement.

Some were even proudly brandishing the tools of their trade, such as screwdrivers, wheel-spanners, monkey-wrenches, sledgehammers, cement-mixers, chainsaws, half-bricks, rolling-pins, and double-entry bookkeeping manuals emblazoned with 'Urgent' Post-It Notes.

According to Provincial Road Traffic authorities, traffic on the major arterial routes was flowing very smoothly and normally for this time of day, although there appeared to be more pedestrians marching down the N2 freeway into Cape Town than usual.

High in the blustery blue sky over Table Mountain, a traffic reporter calmly advised motorists to consider using an alternative route, such as the N2 freeway to the airport.

On the outskirts of Soweto, a sprawling, dusty township on the outskirts of Johannesburg, eagle-eyed members of the Internal Stability Unit of the South African Police warmed their hands over a barricade of blazing car-tyres, pausing only to exchange warm greetings with ordinary, everyday township residents on their way to the heart of the city's central business district.

In the front seat of a customised armoured vehicle with 400 watt quadraphonic speakers on the roof and floor, an off-duty riot constable idly flipped a cassette tape of 'The Greatest Hits of the Police' on to the second side, thereby inadvertently erasing everything on the first side.

Several stones' throws away, in the heart of Pretoria's historic Paul Kruger Square, a small knot of ordinary, everyday South Africans gathered to change the name of the square to something more appropriate to the current socio-political environment.

After a peaceful and democratic debate, featuring several constructive suggestions from passing civil servants and plainclothes members of the Afrikaner Weerstandsbeweging, the small crowd unanimously agreed that the name should be changed from Paul Kruger Square to Paul Kruger Piazza.

Then, because it was such a nice day, with a mild westerly breeze blowing in from the snow-covered foothills of the Maluti Mountains, the modest cluster of ordinary, everyday South Africans decided to burn a few stray flags and newspapers for warmth before setting off on a casual stroll to the Union Buildings.

Meanwhile, as the strains of the Dr Snuggles theme tune lingered like a sweet fragrance in the normal, everyday air, a newsreader for *Good Morning South Africa* said good morning to South Africa and proceeded to read the news.

'Good morning. Despite calls by the ANC-COSATU-SACP alliance for a massive stayaway and general strike in support of today's massive Rolling Mass Action campaign, hundreds of thousands of South Africans reported for work as usual at the SABC this morning.

'Although spokesmen for some factories and offices across the country have reported isolated incidents of people not turning up for work, this has been attributed to the fact that it is a Monday, and anyway, a lot of people tend to go on leave at this time of year.

'Also, some people are away on routine outside training courses, while several thousand are believed to be on "Sabbatical" for a couple of days. Besides which, many people phoned in to say they are feeling a bit fluey. Gezundheit.

'We will now cross briefly to the Union Buildings in Pretoria, where thousands and hundreds of ordinary, everyday South Africans have stopped to admire the statues on their way to work. OK, that's it. Will you please stop watching television and go to work now.'

## *How to roll your own Mass Action campaign*

A Rolling Mass Action campaign, as opposed to a Stationary Mass Action campaign, is any campaign designed to bring traffic, commerce, industry, and the Government to a standstill on any given day of the non-working week.

Also known as 'The Leipzig Option', on account of the growing number of South Africans who have emigrated to Leipzig, the Rolling Mass Action campaign has been hailed as one of the most effective methods of installing a truly representative democratic government without wasting everyone's time on an election.

Unlike elections, Rolling Mass Action campaigns are open to anyone who would like to join in, and even if you wouldn't, you're still very welcome. To participate in a Rolling Mass Action campaign, simply roll up at your nearest major traffic intersection on Mass Action Day.

Bring placards, banners, posters, pickets, T-shirts, petitions, bumper-stickers, barricades, boots, badges, flags, matches, and sandwiches. You will also need a map of the proposed route in your area.

Please note that the names of some of the streets, buildings, trees, plants, restaurants, airports, motorways, and national monuments along the route will be subject to change without further notice.

In case of doubt, your nearest impartial United Nations monitor will be able to point you in the direction of the nearest airport. OK, let's get rolling.

## *How to march into a city centre on a so-called public freeway*

Etched in blue on national and provincial roadmaps, designated by diamond-shaped reflective markers, South Africa's public freeways offer quick and convenient connection between one public freeway and another.

Once you have found your way on to the freeway network, it is possible to travel perpetually between the N1, the N3, the M2 East and the 'Ben Schoeman' without ever actually getting anywhere.

For this reason, freeways can play a highly symbolic role in a Rolling Mass Action campaign, with thousands of people taking to the on-ramps in protest against some of the more restrictive laws still remaining on the statute books.

An example is paragraph 4 (i) of sub-section 2 (b) of the Road Traffic Act and Accompanying Amendments, which states: 'No person bearing an anti-Government poster, placard, or uprooted stop-sign shall march, stroll, amble, saunter or otherwise proceed on foot down the middle of a public freeway at rush-hour.'

This arbitrary decision, steamrollered on to the statute books without consultation, is yet another example of Government intransigence in the field of pedestrian rights.

In order to drive this point home, a 'freeway de-regulation' campaign should be put into gear as a vital cog in the wheel of any Rolling Mass Action campaign.

Permission to defy the law on pedestrian access to public freeways may be obtained from the nearest bona fide traffic officer along the route.

In terms of an agreement between Provincial Road Traffic authorities, the United Nations, and 40 000 people marching down the middle of the freeway at rush-hour, the

*Stop signs of the times: how to bring the country to a standstill during a Rolling Mass Action campaign.*

following rules and regulations will apply.

Please present petition calling for freeing of the freeways to the traffic officer standing on the off-ramp, along with application for general amnesty for jaywalkers and Jay Naidoo.

1. No person will be permitted to proceed on foot down a public freeway unless there is at least 0,25mm of tread remaining on his or her tackies.

2. Please observe minimum following distance of two feet at all times during protest march on freeway.

3. No hand-signals allowed on freeway, unless you are marching past a bona fide Government building.

4. Please pull over on to the hard shoulder if you have reason to suspect that you are about to develop a blister on your blisters.

5. No personal or 087 calls allowed from yellow SOS phone-booths.

6. Reversing on a freeway is strictly forbidden, so please carry on marching for another 15,2km if you forget to turn off at your designated off-ramp.

7. Do not remove large orange cones from freeway roadwork sites, as they are illegal in terms of the blanket prohibition on carrying pointed objects during a protest march.

8. Please call ahead and book a table for 40 000 if you intend stopping off at a designated freeway rest-stop along the way.

9. It would be appreciated if you refrain from changing the names of towns and cities on overhead destination-markers, as this would tend to confuse and disorientate motorists who are trying to find a way to get off the freeway. On second thoughts, go ahead. It might actually make things easier.

*Please note that it is illegal to wield any pointed item in a threatening manner during a Rolling Mass Action campaign.*

## *How not to file your income tax return as part of a Rolling Mass Action campaign*

Next to not paying traffic fines, not paying bond instalments, and not paying attention to the Deputy Minister of Constitutional Development, not paying income tax for the current tax year is one of the most popular rolling mass activities of any Rolling Mass Action campaign.

'We are sick and tired of taxpayers' money being used by the Government to intimidate and harass innocent people who have not yet sent in their income tax returns,' explained a spokesman for the People's Co-ordinating Committee on Ideologically-Motivated Tax Evasion.

Please note that all voluntary donations to the Committee are fully tax-deductible in terms of section 3 (i) of the Income Tax Act and Accompanying Amendments.

If you would like to play a more active role in the campaign, all you have to do is fill in Form IT 12 (Return of Income: Individual) according to the rules and guidelines prescribed in Form IT 382/P (Income Tax: Information Brochure).

Be sure to complete all sections pertaining to Gross Income Received and/or Accrued, Gross Income Still In the Post But Should Arrive Any Day Now, Share Options Exercised, Share Options Sitting on the Sofa and Watching Television, Sworn Statement of Assets and Liabilities, Censored Statement of Assets and Liabilities, and all Rebates and Deductions Claimed in Respect of Medical and Dental Expenses, Legal Expenses, Illegal Expenses, Tool Allowance, Cultural Weapon Allowance, and Use of Chauffeur-Driven Vehicle to Participate in People's Mass Protest March to the Offices of the Receiver of Revenue.

A representative from the Receiver's office will be on hand to refuse to receive your income tax return, on the grounds that you have not signed the bit declaring that all information contained therein is true and correct to the best of your knowledge.

The official slogan of the anti-tax campaign of the Rolling Mass Action campaign is 'No Taxation Without Representation'. Don't worry. Once you have found an attorney to represent you on charges of gross tax evasion, you should be able to claim a sizeable amount for Legal Expenses.

## *How to occupy a Government building*

According to the Joint Interim Guidelines For a Peaceful and Democratic Mass Action Campaign, Government buildings in most of the major centres in South Africa may be occupied at any time between 8 am and 9.30 am, 9.45 am and 10.50 am, 11.05 am and 12.30 pm, and 2 pm and 3 pm on any day of the week that does not fall on a public holiday or official stayaway.

No occupation of any kind will be allowed during tea-breaks, coffee-breaks, snack-breaks, chat-breaks, smoke-breaks, work-breaks, cake-breaks, and lunch, and any occupying parties who are still in the building at 3.01 pm will be obliged to file for overtime in terms of Civil Service regulations.

Before occupying the Government building of your choice, you will be required to complete a Visitor Application Form at the Security Desk in the foyer. State 'Occupation' under Reason For Visit, 'Occupier' under Occupation, and 'Security Guard' under Person to See.

Don't forget to fill in full name, home address, work and home phone, identity number, tax number, nationality, vehicle registration, political affiliation, three credit references, and estimated time and date of filling in form.

Please use non-writing implement provided on end of chain, as all pens and pencils in your possession will have to be surrendered in terms of the blanket provision on carrying pointed objects during a Mass Action campaign.

When you have completed your form, you will be handed a security sticker which must be displayed in a prominent position on your forehead at all times during your occupation of the building.

Since your planned action will include sitting-in, lying down, stomping along corridors, complaining about the Government, and generally doing everything in your power to obstruct the smooth traffic of bureaucracy, this sticker will play a vital role in distinguishing you from bona fide employees of the Civil Service.

As soon as the other 24 999 participants in the Mass Action campaign have finished filling in their forms, you may proceed in an orderly fashion towards the glass-enclosed security cubicles.

Press the button once only, and pull the door towards you when the green light flashes. Enter the cubicle, and wait for the orange light to flash before pushing the second door away from you.

If the red light flashes and a high-pitched two-note alarm sounds, do not be alarmed. A security guard will be on the scene within minutes. In the meantime, you may occupy the glass-enclosed security cubicle. For security reasons, no toyi-toyiing is permitted in the cubicle, although you are welcome to chant anti-Government slogans once you have finished shouting for help.

Please head directly for the first available lift as soon as you have been released. A marshal will hand you a number. You are to proceed to this floor when the lift is full.

If the lift does not arrive within 45 minutes of pressing the button, it may mean that the power supply has been disconnected as part of a broad campaign for people's power. Or it may mean that the Civil Service is about to go on lunch.

If this is the case, you will find the self-service cafeteria just below the parking garage on the fourth basement level. After lunch, and a brief occupation of the cafeteria in protest at the quality of Government-subsidised food, please proceed back up the stairs to your designated occupational floor.

Now find something to keep yourself occupied. Examples: filing reports, filing nails, filing cabinets, filing Cabinet Ministers, dancing, chanting, watering plants, planting bugs, reading top-secret letters addressed to 'The Occupant', sending urgent inter-departmental memos, trying to find a pen that works, filling in a requisition form for a pen that works, waiting for an official to accept a petition, trying Mnr Smit in Room 312, trying Mnr Jacobs in Room 624, trying Mnr Van Tonder in Room 225, and applying for a job with the Civil Service.

In the event that the Mass Action campaign achieves its goals, you may occupy the fourth chair from the left on the east wing of the lower sub-mezzanine level (Requisitions Department). But first, have another cup of tea and a slice of melktert.

*How to occupy a lift during a Rolling Mass Action campaign.*

## *How to stage a mock trial*

No Rolling Mass Action campaign for peace, justice, and democracy is complete without a 'mock trial' in the renamed public square of your choice. You may choose your mock defendants from a wide range of public figures, including television quizmasters, radio talkshow hosts, Sunday newspaper columnists, Telkom employees, insurance salesmen, and Naas Botha.

But unless you have got all day, it might be more practical to narrow your field down to a few selected civil servants and members of the Cabinet. In the interests of mock justice, it is highly recommended that you allow your mock defendants an opportunity to respond to the charges brought against them.

The following mock summons may be faxed to the relevant defendants a couple of minutes before the trial begins:

MOCK SUMMONS

URGENT FAX FOR: The Mock Defendant

FROM: The Mock Prosecuting Attorney, Department of Mock Justice, Paul Kruger Piazza

Dear The Hon/Prof/Dr/Sir/Mr/Mrs/Madam (Please note that you will be stripped of your title once you have been found guilty of the charges brought against you)

Congratulations! You, The Hon/Prof/Dr/Sir/Mr/Mrs/ Madam, have been personally selected by show of fists to take part in what promises to be one of the most spectacular and exciting exercises in democracy ever to be presented in the history of South Africa!

All you have to do is attend an innovative and mass action-packed 'mock trial', at which you will be asked to answer a variety of charges relating to your role in the history of South Africa.

Yes, it's that simple, The Hon/Prof/Dr/Sir/Mr/Mrs/Madam, and to make it even harder for you to say 'No', we have listed some of these charges hereunder for your perusal:

1. Failing to attend a mock trial despite receiving a personalised invitation.

2. Refusing to hand over the reins of power to legitimate representatives of the next Government, thereby depriving them of valuable pension benefits.

3. Letting go of the reins of your horse while participating in a parade in Paul Kruger Square, thereby causing a traffic obstruction and rolling mass hysteria among spectators.

4. Exceeding the 2,5-hour time limit for opening and/or closing addresses to delegates at Codesa or reasonable facsimile thereof.

5. R1,265,542 (one million, two hundred and sixty-five thousand, and five hundred and forty-two rand only) including 15 per cent VAT. This particular charge relates to your current telephone bill, and may be queried with your local Telkom Area Manager during normal business hours.

Once you have been found guilty on the abovementioned charges, The Hon/Prof/Dr/Sir/Mr/Mrs/Madam, you could stand in line to receive some of the most incredible sentences ever to be handed down in a mock South African courtroom!

These range from an all-expenses-paid two-week holiday

in a luxury caravan park in Witbank, to being locked in a room for three hours with no one but Jay Naidoo for company! All right, make it two-and-a-half hours.

Either way, we are sure that you will not want to turn down the opportunity to be a part of this historic mock trial, The Hon/Prof/Dr/Sir/Mr/Mrs/Madam.

However, if you are unable to attend due to pressure of work or previous commitments, we would be most grateful if you could send us one large signed photograph of yourself, along with a detailed curriculum vitae.

Include all official appointments and previous convictions, such as 'Used to believe in Apartheid many years ago, but don't see why that should be held against me'.

Should you intend defending the charges brought against you, please tick one or more of the following suggested statements from the dock:
☐ I was only following orders.
☐ I was only giving orders.
☐ I hereby declare a general amnesty.
☐ On second thoughts, I hereby declare a State of Emergency.
☐ Phew, thank goodness this is only a mock trial.

Please RSVP by the time you finish reading this, and send no money now. Well, OK, send money. Remember to paste the big bright yellow 'YES, PLEASE!' sticker, or the small off-white 'thanks, but no thanks' sticker, on the outside of the envelope.

Looking forward to meeting you,

The Mock Chief Justice
Rolling Mass Action campaign

Please note that as soon as the mock trial proceedings have been completed, all participants are requested to adjourn to the nearest magistrate's court for a 'real trial' on the following charges: obstructing traffic in a public thoroughfare; deflating tyres of police vehicles; releasing handbrakes of Telkom minibuses parked on downhills, thereby forcing them to become part of a Rolling Mass Action campaign; disturbing the peace; disturbing the democracy; removing Paul Kruger's top hat; repainting the Voortrekker Monument without submitting a tender to the Department of Public Works; interfering with certain species of indigenous plant in the gardens of the Union Buildings; and contempt of court.

Thank you.

# *How To Query Your Telkom Account*

Telkom, not to be confused with 'The Post Office', is a semi-privatised corporation set up by the Government to run the telephone and electronic communications services in a post-Apartheid South Africa. For further information, please contact your nearest Post Office.

Address all correspondence to The Postmaster, The Nearest Post Office, Telkom, South Africa, and remember to enclose a blank postal order to cover any increases in postal fees that may come into effect between the time you pop your letter in the postbox and the time the postman picks it up and hands it to the Postmaster.

Now that Telkom is a commercialised operation run along strict free enterprise principles, consumers will no longer have cause to complain to the Government about the inefficiency, bureaucracy, and surly indifference of telecommunications employees. Instead, please complain directly to Telkom.

You will find the telephone number of your nearest Telkom Area Manager under 'Complaints, General Enquiries, and Perpetual Engaged Signal' in the current edition of your regional telephone directory. To obtain a current edition of your regional telephone directory, stand in the queue and hand your telephone directory voucher to the person standing in front of you.

Then go outside and use the telephone directory that has been chained to the callbox to prevent people stealing the callbox after they have stolen the telephone directory. Do not attempt to use the callbox.

If your enquiry concerns the amount owing on your telephone account, you may apply in person for prompt and courteous service. Ask the lady dipping the koeksister into her tea behind the dried protea arrangement for a 'Prompt and Courteous Service' application form. This will take approximately three weeks to process.

In the meantime, you are advised to take a couple of days off work, get yourself a good selection of novels and a hamper of sandwiches, and go to the back of the Telephone Account Enquiries and Complaints queue. Thank you, and please call again.

## *How to tell your telephone number from the amount owing on your telephone account*

According to independent research by Telkom's Customer Relations Department, telephone account enquiries account for up to 97 per cent of Telkom's daily complaints workload.

Of the remaining 42 per cent, 20 per cent are related to the way Telkom employees drive their company minibuses, and 16,5 per cent to the fact that Telkom employees do not appear to be very good at arithmetic.

Because of the disproportionately high rate of telephone account queries flowing into Post Offices on a daily basis, except for Sundays, Public Holidays, Saturdays after 1 pm, and Lunch, Telkom's Workload Alleviation Department has decided to lay down the following guidelines for people wishing to query their telephone account.

1. Telephone accounts are made up on a monthly basis by Telkom's Creative Accounting Department, using a patented system of 'Random Number Generation' linked to a sophisticated computer network.

Even so, mistakes do sometimes occur, and you may find that the figure on your telephone account is an actual reflection of the amount owing. If you suspect that this may be the case, please point it out when you get to the front of the queue, and a thorough departmental investigation will be conducted.

In the meantime, you will be reassigned a figure at random from a book of logarithm tables. You may now return to the back of the queue.

2. In accordance with Telkom's policy of always giving the customer the benefit of the doubt in any dispute over a

telephone account payment, you may elect to pay your telephone number if it appears to be a lesser figure than the amount owing on your telephone account.

Simply fill in your telephone number in the little blank box on your cheque, and the computer will calculate what the amount should read in words. You may use more than one cheque if necessary.

3. To avoid inconvenience caused by the disconnection of your telephone service, please make sure that your account is paid on or before the due date. Due to postal delays, strikes, and computer error, this date will usually have expired two weeks before you receive your account.

However, this will only be accepted as an excuse if you work for Telkom.

4. If you are concerned that your monthly telephone account will not arrive in time to be paid before your telephone is disconnected, you may make use of Telkom's convenient Telephone Account Payment Reminder Service.

For a nominal monthly charge, a friendly and efficient Telkom employee will telephone and remind you to pay your nominal monthly charge before reminding you to pay your telephone account, or else.

If you are not home to receive your reminder, please contact Telkom immediately to remind them to try again. Please note that this service is provided without prejudice to Telkom's right to cut off your telephone anyway.

5. Although Telkom welcomes telephone account enquiries as part of its ongoing commitment to giving Telkom employees something interesting to do between tea and lunch, it would be beneficial to all concerned if subscribers took the time to analyse their telephone habits before habitually complaining that their telephone accounts

cannot possibly be as high as they are.

For instance, do you frequently find yourself dialling wrong numbers or crossed lines? If so, this could account for as much as half of your account, as wrong numbers and crossed lines are now charged at 150 per cent of the SRRPM (Standard Random Rate Per Minute). A 10 per cent surcharge will apply if at least one of the parties on the crossed line is Dr Paul, the well-known telephone sex therapist.

Do you hear the constant sound of rushing or gurgling water in the background whenever you use your telephone? If so, your telephone is probably being 'tapped', an exclusive Telkom service billed at R120 per litre or part thereof, plus labour.

Do you make regular use of Directory Enquiries, Repair Services, Trunk Calls, Test-a-Number, Dial-a-Conference, Ships at Sea, and Time? If so, you should really find something more interesting to read than the green pages at the front of your regional telephone directory.

6. If you would like to obtain interesting, up-to-the-minute information on a variety of subjects ranging from sex to astrology to Van der Merwe jokes to sex to rugby to cooking to sex to horse-racing to pop music to sex, please dial '087' and the first seven digits you can think of after you've thought of sex.

087 calls cost as little as R0,87 per second, and you could stand in line to win a cash prize of R2 000 000 (two million rand and nought cents only), with incremental bonus for every 15 minutes you stay on the line.

This money could go a long way towards the payment of your monthly telephone account, so don't delay, call 087 and seven digits today.

This has been a public service announcement brought to

you by Telkom, the nation's leading supplier of 087 technology and telephones with 0, 8, and 7 on the dial.

Thank you, and please call again.

*All-purpose Telkom telephone account enquiry and complaint form*
*(Please fill in neatly and return to back of queue)*

To Whom It May Or May Not Concern,
Consumer Complaints Department,
Telephone Accounts Division,
Exorbitant Amounts Sub-Division,
Lower Basement Level,
Telkom,
The Post Office,
South Africa

Sir,

I wish to register a complaint concerning my telephone account for the month of ... (fill in month and year). Normally, my account amounts to ... (fill in average amount of telephone account).

However, the amount indicated on the attached account is ................................................
................................ (fill in amount, using extra sheet of paper if necessary) ....................
........................................................

I do not believe that this amount is an accurate reflection of the telephone usage in my household during the month in question, as (please tick one only):

▫ My telephone was already cut off by mistake three months ago, and you haven't sent anyone around to fix it.

▫ I keep my telephone locked in a double-insulated combination safe in the garden-shed whenever I am not at home, and I only use it once every evening to participate in radio talkshows on the desirability of commercialising certain branches of the Civil Service.

▫ I recently installed an 087 Guard to prevent people from making unauthorised 087 calls on my telephone. The 087 Guard assures me that he has not been making 087 calls, so the only possible explanation must be that someone else's 087 calls have erroneously been billed to my account.

I would be very grateful if an urgent and thorough commission of inquiry could be launched into the above account by the person in charge of the computer responsible for the error.

I hereby declare that I am prepared to give evidence by telephone if called on to do so, and I therefore enclose a cheque for the amount of ............................
........................ (fill in amount, using extra decimal point if necessary) ........................
.... to cover my telephone account and lunch for the commission.

In the event that the aforesaid commission finds that there has been an error in the calculation of the abovementioned telephone account, I hereby agree to pay the shortfall within 30 (thirty) days of receipt of revised account.

Thanking you in advance,
Yours sincerely,

The Complainant

*Cut down on soaring telephone bills by installing a Telkom-approved 087 Phone Guard today.*

# *Boerewors Of The Vanities*
## *The Secret Diaries of Jani Allan*

*Tue, Feb 9:* Interviewed a Mr Eugene Terre'Blanche for my sparkling-as-ever celebrity interview column this morning. Apparently, he's the leader of some or other political organisation beginning with an 'A' — will have to check on that, plus the correct spelling of his name.

Is it Eugene with an 'e' or Eugene with a 'u', and if so, is there one of those little umlaut things on top of the 'u'? As a professional journalist, I am concerned about such details.

Speaking frankly and off-the-record, I must confess that I found this Mr Terre'Blanche to be an immensely boring interview subject, particularly the way he kept boring into me with his boring blue eyes. As for his voice, all I can say is that I have heard more melodious snores. I shall have to liven up the story with a few interesting metaphors and some discreet hyperbole.

Went out for fettucini with Alfredo, a really dishy Italian airline pilot. Never in my wildest fantasies did I ever imagine I would have such an unbelievable evening with such an incredible hunk. It's just as well that our relationship is entirely professional.

Had three Italian kisses for dessert, feel like blimp, off to aerobics first thing tomorrow.

*Wed, Feb 10:* Telephoned Mr Terre'Blanche today to check on spelling of his name.

Can you believe it, he wasn't in. Secretary tried to help, but she could only spell in Afrikaans.

Well, I am afraid I can't sit around all week waiting for Mr Terre'Blanche to phone me back, so I have arranged another appointment for tomorrow. Let's just hope it's a quick one.

Went out for shrimp cocktail with Sven, a really charming Norwegian submarine captain. What a dreamboat, just a pity he doesn't speak a word of English. Must interview him for my column sometime.

Did I get a fright this evening — stood on bathroom scale and saw that I had put on 2,5 kilograms. Then I realised that I had forgotten to take my make-up off.

Spent a few hours alone in bed, listening to Mr Terre'Blanche's voice on my tape-recorder. As a professional journalist, I want to be sure that I quote him accurately. Must remember to put fresh batteries in for tomorrow.

*Thu, Feb 11:* Woke up with really sore head. Couldn't work out what it was, until I realised I had been sleeping with the tape-recorder underneath my pillow all night.

Had this crazy dream that I was riding in the back seat of an ox-wagon down a big street in some major city, wearing khaki and waving at thousands of people standing on the pavement. You won't believe who was sitting next to me: Sven, the Norwegian submarine captain. Thank goodness we are just good friends.

Met Mr Terre'Blanche at his office in Pretoria this morning. He was very cordial, and said I did not need to call him 'Mr' all the time. 'OK, Terre'Blanche,' I said, and we got down to business.

He handed me his business card, which was just as well, as I had forgotten to bring my notebook and the batteries in my tape-recorder had expired while I was listening to the interview in my car. So had the tape.

Terre'Blanche said he had booked a table for two at an

intimate restaurant in a quiet part of the city, so would I please hurry up and ask my questions because he didn't want to keep the person waiting. I told him not to worry, we could do it on the phone tomorrow.

Went out for Bratwurst with Fritz, an up-and-coming Bavarian landscape painter.

Thank goodness I can't stand the sight of him.

*Fri, Feb 12:* Eugene. Eugene, Eugene, Eugene. EUGENE. I sit at my computer terminal and type his name over and over, until I am satisfied that I can do it with my eyes closed.

As a professional journalist, I believe in doing all that I can to create the illusion that I am working. The column has to be in by 11 am. It is now 10.17 am and 20 seconds. The Chief Sub-editor has just looked over my shoulder to see how I am getting on.

'I'm on 452 words,' I tell him, not mentioning that they are all Eugene. My heart is fluttering like a butterfly caught in a device used to catch butterflies.

Small beads of perspiration are breaking through my secondary layer of Max Factor No. 7 Foundation Base With Built-in Perspiration Inhibitor. I feel a strange tingling sensation in my goosepimples. What am I going to do? It is 11.37 am and 40 seconds.

Oh well, I suppose I could just dash off a few words about the face, the beard, the eyes, the uniform, the voice ... a sort of 'impressionistic' fantasy piece with lots of italics and gratuitous punctuation.

But first, I will telephone Eugene at his home in Ventersdorp, a small maize-farming town in the far Western Transvaal. As a professional journalist, I have always believed in maintaining a certain distance between myself and my subjects.

Anyway, I just want to hear his voice for purposes of a quick metaphoric comparison. Boy, am I exhausted. It is 11.22 pm, and I have just handed my column to the Chief Sub-editor. He seemed rather agitated, but fortunately I could not hear a thing, as my ear had gone all numb from the telephone.

*Sat, Feb 13:* Had enormous row with Roger, a rowing coxman from Oxford. He said he had waited outside my flat all night, and had even looked through the keyhole at one stage to see if I was at home. What nonsense! As if it is possible to see anything of interest through a tiny keyhole.

I told him it was not my fault that I had forgotten about our dinner-date, and anyway, if it hadn't been for the British and their stupid colonial wars against the Transvaal and Orange Free State Republics, South Africa would not be in the mess it was in today.

Went shopping at Sandton City this morning. Fantastic sale at Safrics — bought three-piece khaki slack-suit with matching leather bandolier for carrying lipstick and stuff.

*Sun, Feb 14:* Had mysterious telephone call from Eugene this morning. All he wanted to know was whether I knew what day it was.

'Yes, it's Sun, Feb 14,' I replied, after consulting my secret diary. Eugene said he would call again during the week, as he had to rush out and buy an extra 650 copies of today's paper for his files.

I wonder what he thinks of the story. One gets very little feedback in this business.

This afternoon, 14 dozen long-stemmed red roses and a magnum of French Champagne were hand-delivered to my doorstep. I was overwhelmed with paroxysms of bliss and ecstasy, until I read the note and realised that they were for my room-mate.

I am going to have to speak to her about this. It's the third time this week, and we are running out of vases. One thing's for sure. She can pay the water bill this month.

*Wed, June 15:* Had lunch with Euge at one of Ventersdorp's classiest maize restaurants. Everything on the menu is made from mealies or mealie by-products.

Wasn't hungry, so I just ate the menu, which was made from a mealie's husk.

Euge ordered a huge rump steak, which they had to import from the steakhouse across the road. As a professional journalist, I believe it is important to maintain contact with one's contacts. Even if you do not get a story out of them every time, it is still worth all the effort and schlepp of travelling to Ventersdorp three or four times a week.

In any case, I think I may be on to something really big. Apparently, the newspaper I work for is Government-controlled. That would explain a lot, such as why the pay is so lousy. Must remember to ask Euge which Government he means, specifically.

*Fri, July 23:* Boy, am I annoyed. I spent all of last night working on my front-page exclusive about the way certain newspapers are secretly controlled and funded by the Government, and now it looks as if my newspaper is not going to be able to use it.

The Chief Sub-editor said it was an excellent piece of typing, but I did not have enough 'proof' to support my allegations. Ha! Little do these people realise that I have in my possession an actual copy of a newspaper entitled 'The

Government Gazette'. Must remember to return it to Eugie as soon as possible.

This afternoon, as I was strolling down to the canteen to get some Perrier Water, I overheard a bunch of journalists discussing an alleged 'intimate relationship' between a prominent local personality and a leading figure on the political scene.

Naturally, they stopped talking as soon as I approached. They are obviously aware of my reputation and know that I would be able to get to the bottom of such a story in no time at all. But really, who would be interested?

*Sun, Aug 21:* I am so embarrassed! While riding with Eugie in the lush green hill-country around Bronkhorstspruit, an important maize-milling centre near Ventersdorp, I momentarily lost my balance and fell into the spruit after which Bronkhorstspruit is named.

Eugie was very apologetic when he returned to pick me up half-an-hour later. He said this kind of thing often happened when two people were riding the same horse, and that I could sit in front for a while to make up for it. I must admit that Eugie is a terrific equestrian, albeit a little on the heavy side.

The horse was so exhausted after our three-hour tour of historic battle-sites in the Bronkhorstspruit area, that we were forced to dismount for a few hours in the middle of a secluded mealiefield. Thank goodness I remembered to bring my notebook, as Eugie gave me some really great quotes for an in-depth article I am doing on why the AWB should be running the country.

As a professional journalist, I believe one should be in possession of all the relevant facts before forming an objective opinion on a major political issue.

However, I have not yet decided whether to wear the khaki slack-suit with the full-face balaclava or the slinky black-and-red strapless gown with the high-heel jackboots to the inaugural ball.

*Mon, Sep 12:* I am getting increasingly frustrated with the way the Government is controlling the Press in this country. Of the 114 exclusive articles I have submitted on Eugene Terre'Blanche thus far, only 42 have been used, and 12 of those were hidden away on the back page.

This is hardly the way to treat one of the country's top investigative reporters, and it is certainly no way to treat me. After all, I have personally gone out of my way to get the inside story on Eugene Terre'Blanche, willingly sacrificing my free time to peel away the layers of myth and legend that lie behind the illusion of reality.

I am convinced that one day the truth will emerge, but in the meantime, I am coming under increasingly heavy pressure from Eugene himself. I really do think he should go on some sort of diet.

Oh well, at least I have made up my mind about one thing. The Union Buildings.

That dull sandstone exterior has simply got to go. I quite like the statues, however, and it should not be too difficult to update the one of the bloke sitting on the horse.

*Sat, Oct 22:* Went out for a Prego with Stephano, Alberto, Romano, Ricardo, Alphonso, Leonardo, Avocado and Figmento this evening. They are members of a small Portuguese television crew who have been sent out here to do a documentary series on 'Top Nightspots of Krugersdorp and the Far West Rand'.

Boy, was I relieved. I had thought for a moment that they

were planning to do a major investigative report on Eugene Terre'Blanche and the AWB. As a professional journalist, I am constantly bothered by the thought that some other professional journalist will attempt to steal my story and pass it off as his or her own.

However, I am quite happy to see what I can do to accommodate these Portuguese people, as long as some of them do not mind sleeping in the lounge. Due to the communist onslaught and the Government, South Africa does not always enjoy a very good image in the overseas media, and I feel I should do my bit to help push all the violence and political turmoil off the front pages for a change.

Must speak to Eugie; he should be able to come up with a couple of ideas.

*Wed, Nov 16:* Went out to the historic Paardekraal Monument with Eugie this evening. It really is an awe-inspiring sight, standing there as tall and proud as a beacon in the moonlight.

The monument itself also looked quite interesting, but unfortunately it was closed. Thank goodness the Portuguese television crew arrived in time to force the lock open with a crowbar.

They took some really fantastic footage of Eugie declaring war on the Government, but unfortunately none of it came out because the lighting cameraman had forgotten to bring the lights.

Just as well that a member of the South African Police happened to be passing by on a routine patrol, although the Portuguese television crew had already gone back to Portugal by the time the policeman shone his torch on us and demanded to know what we were doing in the grounds of a designated national monument at two o'clock in the morning.

Thank goodness we were only doing the goosestep.

*Thu, Nov 17:* I am devastated! I am writing this on the back of a cigarette box, as I have just realised that I left my secret diary at the Paardekraal Monument last night!

If it falls into the wrong hands, I just don't know what I will do. Hang on ... I'll sue! That's right, I'll sue the underpants off anyone who dares to mention a word about me and any other person I may have had fleeting contact with in the course of my duties as a professional journalist, particularly if I have always considered the aforesaid person to be a repulsive pig.

In the meantime, I am catching the first available flight to London. I believe they are having a fantastic sale on dowdy black dresses and sensible shoes at Harrods.


# *How To Find Your Place In The Sun On Durban's North Beach On New Year's Day*

Situated on the east coast of South Africa, within walking distance of the Indian Ocean, the tropical port city of Durban has always been a popular holiday destination for South Africans who do not live in Durban.

With its sandy, palm-fringed beaches, sparkling-blue lagoons, friendly natives and rich cultural heritage, the Caribbean island of Barbados is just one of the many alternatives available for those who would like to enjoy a holiday by the seaside, but can't stand the thought of going to Durban for the 17th year in a row.

If you are a Transvaler or a Free Stater, or perhaps a Capetonian on a cultural exchange programme, you may want to bear the following handy hints and guidelines in mind if you are planning to spend Christmas and New Year's Day in Durban.

Since traffic to the city is very heavy at this time of year, it is suggested that you leave home as early as possible, for instance, at 4 am on Republic Day.

Assuming you will be driving to Durban, here is a comprehensive checklist of items you will require before you even think of turning the key in the ignition and roaring on to the motorway:

1. Car, or reasonable facsimile thereof;
2. Intercity motorway route map;
3. Five rand note for buying something at café when you stop to ask man behind counter how to get on to intercity motorway;
4. Family-size bottle of fast-acting headache tablets;
5. Selection of popular music tapes to play on in-car stereo system to divert passengers' attention from the fact that all the holiday traffic seems to be zooming by at an incredible rate on the opposite side of the motorway;
6. Selection of books and comics to read while waiting for AA to tow car out of ditch in motorway island, following unsuccessful attempt to join flow of traffic to Durban;
7. Selection of R2 coins for telephoning neighbour with urgent request to smash open kitchen window and switch off iron;
8. Large plastic rubbish-bag for storing speeding-fines

awarded *en route*;
   9. Big map of Barbados.

Once you have arrived in Durban, it is best to head straight for your beachfront hotel, where a friendly reception clerk will blame the computer for the fact that there is absolutely no record of your booking, and anyway, you were supposed to have checked in six-and-a-half hours ago.

However, if you are prepared to wait for a while, the hotel may be able to put you up for the night in a store-room behind the kitchen with hot and cold dripping water and a nice view of the laundry-chute.

This will be a good time to stretch your weary legs with a casual stroll along the Marine Parade, the colourful beachfront promenade modelled after Rio de Janeiro's legendary 'Copacabana'.

Here, far away from the stresses and strains of South Africa's overcrowded, fast-paced inland cities, you will be able to breathe in the salty ocean air, watch the sun set over the Indian Ocean, and bump into several irritating people from the office whose names you can never remember.

Then it's time to go back to the hotel for a good night's sleep, with a leisurely wake-up call scheduled for 4.30 am. This is to ensure that you have the best possible chance of getting to the beach before it really starts getting crowded.

Please note that it is illegal to spend the night on the beach, unless you can prove that there is absolutely no record of your booking due to a computer error. All other beachgoers should bear in mind that seating on the beach is strictly limited, and lying down is virtually impossible.

Nevertheless, it is possible to secure a good position near the front, as long as you arrive before the sun comes up and the tide rushes in. You will find that the sand gets progressively wetter and thicker as you move towards the front of the beach.

This is in order to make it easier for you to sink the pointy bit of your beach-umbrella into the spot you have chosen to occupy until the first few thousand Transvalers emerge from their tour buses at about 6 am. You do not need to worry about the Free Staters at this stage, as they will still be trying to find the beach.

In the meantime, you should remind yourself that it is the democratic right of all South Africans to make use of the amenities on a public beach. At the same time, there is no denying that certain difficulties can arise when all South Africans attempt to exercise this democratic right at the same time.

The following crowd-control procedures and regulations are therefore recommended in order to ensure that South Africans of all shades enjoy their place in the sun.

1. All persons to wear proper attire when bathing. Any item normally worn as underwear, particularly worn underwear, is considered improper, while it is quite acceptable to wear any item you would not consider wearing as underwear because it is three sizes too small.

2. No one allowed to wear a strap-on shark's fin in the water, as this confuses the sharks.

3. Please watch out for bluebottles in water at all times.

4. Please watch out for beerbottles in water at all times.

5. Due to the ongoing water shortage in the Durban municipal area, no more than 20 litre-bottles of sea-water may be collected per person per day.

6. All minibuses parked on beachfront at high tide will be towed away. Please collect from traffic authorities in Mozambique.

7. Please do not feed the seagulls, as they are quite capable of taking food from your plate themselves.

8. Due to lack of space, no games of football or volley-ball will be allowed on beach. Swingball is permitted only on condition that the length of string to which the ball is attached is no greater than 10cm.

9. Orders and requests from lifeguards are to be obeyed at all times. A system of blasts on a regulation referee's whistle will be used to communicate such orders and requests, according to the following standard code.

*Phree-eep:* You are swimming outside of the red markers. Please move in.

*Phreep-phree-eep:* The area between the red markers is full. Please swim in an upright position only.

*Phreep-phreep-phree-eep:* OK, we're going to move the red markers out another two kilometres. But that's it.

*Phreep-phreep-phreep-phreep:* Tide is coming in. The first 500 people sitting on the beach may now go swimming.

*Phree-eep-phreep-phreep:* Sardines are coming in. Please inhale to allow them to get through.

*Phreep-phreep-phree-eep-eep:* The beach has exceeded 300 per cent of its maximum capacity. Would everyone please stand up and tan in a vertical position.

*Phreep-phreep-phweet-phwew:* Statuesque blonde's tanga bikini-top has come off in sudden swell.

*Phreep-phreep-eep-phreep-phreep-eep:* Please stand aside. Emergency rescue team coming into water to attend to innocent Transvaler who emerged from sudden swell with blonde's bikini-top on head.

*Phreep-eep-phreep-eep-phreep-eep:* Move back please. Man selling samoosas, cold-drinks, ice-creams, curry and rice, vetkoek, boerewors rolls, pap, biltong, koeksisters and ice-cubes trying to get through. Please pay in R50 notes

'Um, maybe we should think about postponing the sardine run until the Transvalers go home, guys.'

only, as man does not carry change.

*Phreep-it-phreep-phreep-phr-phrfffffttt:* You have just kicked beach-sand into a lifeguard's whistle. Please try not to damage any small children's sandcastles on the way down, as their fathers may be watching.

*Phreeeeeeeeeeeep-phreeeeeeeeeeeep-phreeeeeeeeep:* Quick! Everyone get out of the water immediately! The Free Staters have arrived.

For further information on how to enjoy a Christmas holiday in Durban, please contact your nearest branch of the Barbados Government Travel Office. *Phreep.*

# How To Declare War On A Visiting International Celebrity

*A suggested itinerary for movie stars, pop stars, television sex symbols, and anyone else who has always wanted to enjoy a taste of traditional South African hospitality*

*DAY ONE:* Arrive Jan Smuts Airport, bustling, sophisticated gateway to the new improved South Africa. Please note that due to ongoing renovations in the international arrivals section, your flight will be diverted to the parking lot of the nearby Boksburg Pick 'n Pay Hypermarket, from where you will be able to board the first available 'minibus taxi' to Customs and Immigration.

It will not be necessary to fasten your seatbelt, as you will be sitting on the roof-rack. Please join the Visiting International Celebrities queue in the arrivals hall, where a trained post-traumatic stress counsellor will be on hand to answer any questions you may have about South African customs and traditions.

Once you have declared that you have nothing to declare, you will be whisked straight through to the VIP Lounge on the Upper Level, where a reception committee from the International Celebrity Wing of the Azanian Youth Organisation will be waiting to declare war on you.

After a brief Molotov Cocktail party, you will be escorted to your chauffeur-driven armoured-car by a phalanx of security policemen and plainclothes members of the élite State President's Guard. It is not customary to tip on such occasions.

*DAY TWO:* You have an early breakfast meeting scheduled with your publicist, your attorney, and your martial-arts instructor in the spectacular President's Suite of the Sandton Sun Hotel.

Unfortunately, the President will still be sleeping, so your meeting will be moved to the Gazebo Executive Coffee Lounge on the mezzanine level. Don't forget to mention that you are a Visiting International Celebrity, in order to qualify for a seven-and-a-half per cent discount on your second cup of Rooibos Tea.

Rest of day at leisure to wander around the glittering boutiques and speciality stores of the Sandton City shopping-mall. Your concierge will be able to tell you if constitutional negotiations are currently in session, in which case you might want to avoid the rush of foreign dignitaries and fact-finding delegates hoping to pick up a bargain at Katz and Lourie.

*DAY THREE:* After your early morning wake-up call, which will take the form of a brick hurled through your window by protesting members of the Boere Bevrydigingsbeweging, it's off to the glittering studios of M-Net Cable Television for the taping of this week's episode of *Revue Plus*. You will be the guest victim.

Please remember to sign your unconditional disclaimer form at the reception desk, and be sure to hand over all dangerous weapons to the security guard on duty. A public relations representative will escort you to your chair on the middle of the sound-stage.

You are kindly urged to refrain from struggling while your arms and legs are strapped in. The interview will now begin. Enjoy.

*DAY FOUR:* Today you are booked on a 10-minute grand tour of the Cultural and Architectural Highlights of the Johannesburg Central Business District, including the Smal Street Mall, the Carlton Centre, and the magnificent neo-classical Rand Supreme Court, where you will be applying for an urgent interdict to prevent the screening of certain segments of *Revue Plus*.

You are then scheduled to address an international media conference in the Grand Ballroom of the towering Johannesburg Sun Hotel. Please note that the start of the conference may be delayed by up to two hours, depending on the number of media representatives who are able to make it into the hotel lobby without being mugged.

Then it's back to the Rand Supreme Court for a mass interdict against several Sunday newspaper columnists. Please wait your turn in the queue.

*DAY FIVE:* Break away from the urban jungle today for the romance and excitement of the African bushveld at its most raw and primitive. You will be staying at a secluded private game-lodge on the borders of the world-renowned Kruger National Park.

At last, a chance to be yourself, unwind, and soak up the blazing sun in the company of wild animals, rugged game-rangers, and television crews dangling out of chartered helicopters just above the tree-tops. A qualified make-up team will be on hand to cover up your more prominent insect bites.

Don't forget to bring along a cushion for tonight's three-hour moonlit game-drive, the highlight of which is almost certain to be the brutal murder of a helpless antelope by a pack of savage hyena. After a gourmet meal of curried venison back at the camp, it's off to bed for a few hours' rest before your 4 am wake-up call and optional 4.30 am game-drive.

Your game-ranger will be happy to provide you with your recommended daily dose of anti-malaria tablets. Valium and other leading tranquillisers are available at a nominal charge.

*DAY SIX:* Experience traditional South African hospitality at its finest at a lavish potjiekos reception in the grounds of the Union Buildings, Pretoria.

The Minister of Foreign Affairs will be your host and cook, unless Codesa or a reasonable facsimile thereof is in session. If this is the case, you will find full instructions under the three-legged cast-iron pot.

Don't forget to try a glass or two of traditional South African 'Mampoer', or clear peach brandy. You will find it in the bottle marked 'Lighter Fuel'.

On your way back to your Johannesburg hotel, you may wish to call at your embassy in Waterkloof, where the deputy under-secretary in charge of Visiting International Celebrities will be able to supply you with a schedule of emergency airlifts. Please book early, as space is limited.

*DAY SEVEN:* Your last full day in this fascinating and challenging country. You have a working brunch lined up with some leading members of the International Celebrity Absolution Committee of the Azanian Youth Organisation, who will consider modifying their declaration of war to a declaration of malicious intent on receipt of a small donation to the political organisation of their choice.

Please explain exactly what you are famous for, as the Azanian Youth Organisation does not always have the time to watch *Revue Plus* or flip through the pages of *You* Magazine. After signing your autograph in the lower right corner of a few blank cheques, it's off to the dazzling casino resort of Sun City, Bophuthatswana, where you will be able to put your clothes, jewellery, and personal accessories up for charity auction after losing heavily at Blackjack.

Then it's a quick flight back to Johannesburg for your farewell party at the awesome Sandton mansion of multi-millionaire celebrity host Douw Steyn. Please remember to wear your gold-plated name-tag, as the main ballroom can accommodate up to 350 visiting international celebrities at once.

This evening will also be your last opportunity to purchase a Visiting International Celebrity all-risks insurance policy, available from the administration office on the mezzanine level. You may pay in foreign currency if you wish.

*DAY EIGHT:* Wave goodbye to sunny South Africa and your newfound acquaintances as you board your convenient direct flight to the international destination of your choice. For a relaxing change of pace, may we suggest Yugoslavia?

## No Easy Trek To Vryheid
### *How to settle for a slightly smaller National Volkstaat, among other things*

*As a member of a breakaway rightwing splinter group consisting of myself and anyone who would be interested in joining me, I have decided to enter into the multi-party constitutional negotiation process.*

*In order to demonstrate my good faith in this regard, I am prepared to settle for a slightly smaller 'national volkstaat', in exchange for the recognition of my sovereign right to leave the country without actually leaving the country.*

*Could you please offer some advice on proclaiming such a volkstaat, and also, how do I get this splinter out of my nose?*

Establishing your own independent national volkstaat within the boundaries of South Africa is as easy as falling off a horse. All you need is a large wall-map of South Africa, a large wall, some drawing-pins, a hammer, a packet of plasters, a black felt-tip marking-pen, and a horse.

Pin map securely to wall, and remove cap from felt-tip marking-pen. Now check to see if map is right side up. The Orange Free State should be to the north of the Cape Province, Transvaal should be to the east of Bophuthatswana, Natal should be to the west of the Indian Ocean, and the Big Hole of Kimberley should be in the

57

*No Easy Trek to Vryheid ... how to find your way to the nearest independent national volkstaat.*

middle of nowhere.

If this is not the case, please check to make sure that you are the right side up. As soon as you have re-mounted your horse, we can begin. The object of the exercise is to outline the boundaries of your projected national volkstaat, with a view to making and gaining realistic concessions during the negotiation process.

It is therefore important to leave some room for hard and fast bargaining, as you will be up against some of the country's most determined and experienced arm-wrestlers.

If you take a good look at the map on the wall, you will notice that the area currently defined as 'South Africa' is located midway between the Atlantic and Indian Oceans, with borders extending as far as Namibia in the southwest, Botswana and Zimbabwe in the north, and Swaziland and Mozambique in the east.

Now grasp your felt-tip marking-pen and trace a continuous line around these boundaries and the entire sub-continental coastal region. Right. This is the volkstaat to which you will claim exclusive and historical title as a sovereign member of an internationally recognised volk.

After several weeks of frank and fruitful negotiation, conducted in a spirit of willing compromise and good neighbourliness, you will be able to go back home with a settlement for a slightly smaller national volkstaat consisting of your home, your front and back garden up to and including the electric security fence, your swimming-pool, the bit of municipal pavement where you leave your rubbish bags on a Thursday, and your horse.

Please note that these boundaries are subject to re-definition in the event that you change your mind and decide to move back to South Africa.

*I was wondering if you could please expand a little on the concept of the 'Revolving Presidency', as outlined by the State President a while ago. The reason I am asking is that I am concerned about the precise role and functions I will be expected to fulfil when it is my turn to be President.*

In a roundabout way, the concept of the 'Revolving Presidency' represents the most revolutionary alternative to a total surrender of power yet devised by South Africa's constitutional negotiators.

What it means is that, instead of one President being allowed to remain in office long enough to abuse his authority and lead the country into social and economic ruin, other Presidents will also be given a turn every now and again.

These Revolving Presidents will be drawn from the ranks of the various political parties, and will serve according to a strict roster to be drawn up by a special constitutional steering committee and displayed in a prominent position on the fridge door at all times.

Each President will serve a maximum of four consecutive States of Emergency, and no President will be allowed to pass a law compelling any other President to take over before it is his turn.

Presidents wishing to swap their terms of office with other Presidents will only be allowed to do so for a very good reason, such as 'pre-booked timeshare accommodation for whole family at Umhlanga Rocks, don't want to disappoint them' or 'feeling a bit fluey ... will do double-shift to make up for it, if that's OK by you'.

Under normal circumstances, the Presidency will be revolved on a basis of diametric opposites, so that a President with liberal democratic leanings will always be replaced by a President with rightwing autocratic leanings, unless the liberal democratic President becomes a raving rightwing autocrat while serving his term of office.

In that case, the concept of the 'Revolving Presidency' is likely to be abandoned, and we'll just have to wait for the next revolution.

*I am a white South African male of 18 years of age, with no physical or mental problems aside from being a white South African male of 18 years of age. As a result, I have been instructed to report for compulsory military service in terms of the Defence Act of 1957, and Amendments.*

*Unfortunately, on the day I am supposed to report for military service, I already have a prior appointment to sit around the house all day picking my nose and listening to heavy metal music.*

*I have therefore decided to become a Conscientious Objector, and was wondering if you could tell me how I go about doing this, and also, how you spell 'Conscientious'.*

Military Service, sometimes referred to as 'conscription', is one of the areas currently under investigation by Codesa's Non-Working Group 2. For some time, it has been felt that the current system of National Service is unfair and discriminatory, inasmuch as it confines the right to Conscientious Objection to a small sub-minority of the South African population.

Many people believe that South Africans of all creeds, races, and sexes should have the right to object to serving in the South African Defence Force if they feel like it. Until this serious imbalance in the law is redressed, the South African Defence Force has advised that exemption from Military Service will only be granted in the following cases:

1. Person objects to serving in any capacity in South African Defence Force on the grounds that he is already a

serving member of the military wing of a bona fide political organisation, other than the National Party;

2. Person objects to serving in any capacity in South African Defence Force on the grounds that he is morally opposed to the policies of the current Government;

3. Person objects to serving in any capacity in South African Defence Force on the grounds that he may be called upon to depose the current Government;

4. Person objects to serving in any capacity in South African Defence Force on the grounds that he may be called upon to take action against a person who objects to serving in any capacity in South African Defence Force;

5. Person objects to serving in any capacity in South African Defence Force on the grounds that he is the only person to have bothered reporting for compulsory military service in terms of the Defence Act of 1957, and Amendments.

*After careful analysis of the political options available to South Africans, as well as a thorough study of the pension plans available to politicians, I have decided to make myself available for election to Parliament.*

*Can you give me some practical advice in this regard, and also, now that I come to think of it, is there still such a thing as Parliament?*

With non-racial, multi-party elections for a national constituent assembly just around the corner from the Houses of Parliament, South African democrats of all political persuasions are gearing themselves up for what has already been billed as 'South Africa's first non-racial, multi-party elections for a national constituent assembly'.

For the first time in history, the elections will be held on a basis of 'universal suffrage', which means that all South

Africans will be able to share the blame for electing the Government.

If you are a bona fide South African citizen of voting age or older, you are more than welcome to put yourself up as a candidate for a registered political party. No particular qualifications are required, although you will need a sworn certificate confirming that you are of sound mind and do not have a criminal record worth mentioning.

You will then be summonsed to appear in a court of law for a brief formal procedure known as 'nomination'. You will not be asked to plead, although you may be asked to shake hands with your opponent for half-an-hour or so, while the photographer from the local knock 'n drop newspaper attempts to diagnose the persistent failure of his flash to flash.

Then it's time to go out and win the hearts and minds of the registered voters in your constituency. Armed with signed posters, pamphlets, manifestos, badges, koeksisters, carnations, promises, and panic buttons, you will wander from door to door in an increasingly desperate attempt to find someone who is prepared to open the outer security door and enter into an argument.

This practice is known as 'canvassing', and is regarded by political analysts as the only sure method of gauging the political leanings of potential voters. By paying close attention to security systems and guard dogs while waiting for The Householder to ignore the buzzer, you will be able to get a good idea of your chances of qualifying for a national constituent assembly pension plan.

Use the following 'Canine Canvassing' table to determine your likely support base:
* Savage Rottweiler with studded leather collar and drooling fangs, triple-locked security gate with

'Hello, I represent the Peaceful and Democratic Party, and I was wondering if I could count on at least one of your votes...'

overhead infra-red sensor, video intercom and razor-wire on walls and roof: *Moderates*.
* Barely visible chihuahua quivering behind khakibos, hand-carved railway sleeper gate with peephole and splinters: *Conservatives*.
* Black Labrador wagging tail, small padlock on wrought-iron gate, tastefully-integrated spikes on garden wall: *Liberals*.
* Two off-white Maltese Poodles yapping at each other in frustrated aggression, concrete wall painted to look like brick wall, burglar-alarm warning-sign in three official languages: *Far Right*.
* Demented Border Collie herding ants, gap-toothed wooden picket-fence, low brick wall overgrown with creepers: *Far Left*.
* No dog, gates wide open, disconnected security system: *Left South Africa*.

# *Just When You Thought It Was Safe To Go Swimming*
*A practical guide to keeping your swimming-pool in almost sparkling condition*

From the air above Johannesburg and the Pretoria-Witwatersrand-Vereeniging triangle, the sight of hundreds of sapphire-blue swimming-pools glittering in suburban backyards has always been a sure sign of homecoming for the patriotic South African who has been travelling the world in search of somewhere else to live.

It is only when you are once again standing in your own suburban backyard, that you begin to realise that the 'glittering sapphire-blue' colour of other people's swimming-pools is an optical illusion caused by the diffraction of ultra-violet light rays and the fact that you are wearing cheap sunglasses.

According to a confidential report by the South African Bureau of Swimming-Pool Standards, the standard colour of a South African swimming-pool is officially defined as 'Stagnant Suburban Swimming-Pool Green, With Traces of Gritty Black Stuff Floating Around the Edges'.

In scientific terms, this is the natural result of the prolonged exposure of bonded hydrogen and oxygen molecules to air, as well as the fact that the house-sitter forgot to backwash the pool or put chlorine in for the last six weeks.

This is nothing to worry about, unless you are planning to put your house on the market while waiting for your Australian residence application to be approved.

In that case, the following Pool Maintenance Programme is guaranteed to have your pool looking sapphire-blue and glittering within months.

Remember, a sparkling, crystal-clear pool can add thousands of rand to the value of your property, as well as making it much easier to locate any pets that may have gone missing while you were away.

The first step in your programme is to get hold of a 'chemical testing-kit' which you will use to determine the 'Optimum pH Balance' of the water in your swimming-pool. If there is no water in your swimming-pool, you may skip this step.

Chemical-testing kits are available from the swimming-pool department of any major hardware store, or you may simply drag the long pole with the net along the bottom of the pool until you think you are able to distinguish your kit from the discarded beer bottles left over from the house-sitter's farewell party.

Then it's time to begin sorting out the p's from the H's.

## *How to get the pH balance right*

According to a recent scientific survey of a bunch of people standing around a pool with beers in their hands, many pool-owning householders neglect elementary pool maintenance because it sounds like such a schlepp, and in any case, everyone knows that the main reason for spending R30 000 on a swimming-pool is the fact that it saves you having to fill your dog's drinking-bowl with water every few days.

Many people are also under the erroneous impression that you need a Master's Degree in Chemical Engineering to 'test the pH balance and stuff like that, as if it's going to make any difference to the dog'.

As a matter of fact, a simple Honours Degree will suffice, and tests have shown that nine out of ten dogs prefer their pool-water to taste of optimally-balanced pH. The tenth dog unfortunately doesn't have a pool.

But what exactly is pH, and how do you get it to balance, as if it's going to make any difference? Well, pH is short for 'Ph.D in Chemical Engineering', and it refers to the delicate balance between the microscopic particles that make the water in your pool look clean and crystal-clear, and those that make it feel wet when you jump in.

To measure pH, remove the little plastic lid from the big vial on your chemical testing-kit, and fill it with pool-water

*Testing the pH level of your pool: time to add a little acid.*

to the line marked 'When'. Rinse well and repeat. Now get out of the pool, taking care not to swallow too much water, and hold the big vial up to the light.

If you do not see anything but leaves and small insects, move to another part of the pool and try again, or just fill with water from nearest tap. You will now need the small dropper-bottle marked '2' in your chemical testing-kit. Unscrew top and squeeze exactly five drops of number 2 into big vial, substituting with Tabasco Sauce if you run out.

Shake vigorously and repeat, this time with lid on vial. Allow to settle. You should now be able to determine the pH balance of your pool-water by comparing the colour of the water in the vial with the colours in the control panel alongside.

Your optimum colour is bright orange, with a pH level of 7,2 on the random measurement scale. If this is the case, please repeat test to eliminate the possibility that you have been cheating.

All right. If the colour in the vial is cream-soda green, licorice black, bubblegum pink, stale-beer yellow, beetroot red, or 'don't know, but wouldn't want to drink it', you are now ready to take a deep breath, hold your nose, and proceed to the second stage of your Pool Maintenance Programme. Shock Treatment.

## *How to shock treat your pool*

*Warning:* Shock treatment of a backyard suburban swimming-pool is a highly complicated emergency procedure, and should not be attempted by any person who can think of a reasonable excuse for putting it off until the next day.

If it already is the next day, here is a checklist of the things you will need:
1. Long garden hosepipe;
2. Balaclava;
3. Wetsuit with snorkel and flippers;
4. Chemical testing-kit;
5. Neighbour with optimally pH-balanced pool.

Ready? OK.

The first and most vital step in the procedure is to get rid of all the water that is currently occupying your pool. This may sound like a drastic measure, but it is the only practical alternative to 'putting chlorine in', 'adjusting the acid/alkaline content', and a whole lot of other technical things you don't want to know about.

So just put on your wetsuit now and dive into the pool and pull out the plug.

Since the average suburban swimming-pool holds approximately 60 000 litres of chemically-imbalanced water, you will need 60 000 empty one-litre milk bottles, obtainable from your nearest glass-recycling depot or neighbour who has been away on a world cruise and forgot to cancel deliveries.

As soon as the bottles are full, your pool will be empty, and it will be time to move on to the next step. At this point, many people want to know what they are supposed to do with the 60 000 bottles of turgid pool-water occupying the area where their garden used to be.

There are several possibilities, but in view of the fact that water is such a scarce commodity, it is perhaps best to seal the bottles, lock them in a spare room, and save them for a rainy day. But don't worry about that now.

Having emptied your pool, you will notice that the

bottom is covered with a thick carpet of assorted leaves, twigs, creepy-crawlies, and house-sitter's girlfriends' bikini-tops.

Although it may appear to be an arduous and daunting task, you should immediately roll up your sleeves, rub your hands, and go and find some bloke who will be prepared to sweep the bottom of the pool for a nominal fee. Ask him to give you a shout as soon as he is finished, and you will be ready to move on to Phase Three.

*Warning:* Phase Three of your swimming-pool's Shock Treatment programme should only be attempted after midnight, or when your neighbour with the optimally pH-balanced pool is away on holiday. In any case, it is essential that you remember to wear your balaclava over your snorkel when you climb over your neighbour's wall with the long garden hosepipe in your hand.

This will prevent you from being recognised should your neighbour arrive home unexpectedly or be awakened by the automatic motion-detecting security lights and infra-red alarm system. You are unlikely to encounter any real problems, however, as all you have to do is dip one end of the hosepipe into your neighbour's swimming-pool before climbing over the wall again.

Be sure to remove your balaclava before climbing over your own wall with the other end of the garden hosepipe in your hand, as your Rottweiler may not recognise you before attempting to remove the balaclava itself. Now put the other end of the hosepipe into your own empty pool.

Get into pool, and suck on end of hosepipe until you begin to hear gurgling, whooshing noises, similar to those made by 60 000 litres of sparkling blue water being siphoned from your neighbour's swimming-pool through a garden hose at midnight. You may now remove your wetsuit and go back to sleep.

Upon awakening, you will be greeted by the sight of a glittering, crystal-clear pool with a pH balance of 7,2, as well as a neighbour with a baseball bat demanding to know why his own swimming-pool is empty except for a bit of garden hosepipe that leads into your swimming-pool, which is full.

That's why they call it Shock Treatment.

## *How to set the timer on your swimming-pool filter*

Setting the timer on your swimming-pool filter is one of the most crucial tasks you will have to perform if you have any intention of committing yourself to a comprehensive and effective Pool Maintenance Programme.

It is only by accurately setting your timer that you will be able to programme your swimming-pool filter to make a churning noise and do whatever it is supposed to do for an optimum number of hours per day. In turn, your filter will be able to generate the suction necessary to operate your automatic pool-cleaner on the rare occasions when your automatic pool-cleaner hasn't got a big leaf stuck in its mouth.

Contrary to popular opinion, setting the timer on your swimming-pool filter is a simple, straightforward procedure that can be performed in minutes by anyone who knows how to set the timer on a video recorder. There is, however, one crucial difference.

Before you can go about setting the timer on your swimming-pool filter, you have to locate your swimming-pool filter. Try looking in the area of your garden immediately adjacent to the compost heap, the button-

*Before the invention of the automatic swimming-pool cleaner.*

spider colony, and the bulbous, rusting hulk of unidentified scrap metal that you asked the rubble-removal guys to get rid of the last time they came, but they must have forgotten.

Right. The bulbous, rusting hulk of unidentified scrap metal is your swimming-pool filter, and you may now brush away some of the smaller button-spiders in an attempt to find the switch marked 'Timer'. This should be right next to the smaller switch marked 'Timer Override', which should be right next to the big sticker with detailed instructions on how to override the Timer Override in order to set the timer on your swimming-pool filter.

Unfortunately, the detailed instructions on the sticker will have disappeared as a result of a process known as 'progressive chemical evaporation and lack of exposure to anyone even remotely interested in reading instructions'. Don't worry. Here are the detailed instructions, as copied from an interesting booklet entitled 'How to Set the Timer on Your Video Recorder'.

1. Turn on Timer Override switch, and set to 'Off'.
2. Set filter pump switch to 'Timer'.
3. Select programme from TV guide.
4. Manually override 'Standby' switch.
5. Stand by.
6. Using nail on little finger, adjust 24-hour clock on Timer to start at 4.22 am and finish at 22h50 the previous day.
7. Call rubble-removal guys.
8. Stick videotape in slot, press 'Play', and watch three-and-a-half hours of wavy lines and electro-magnetic interference.
9. Throw video recorder into swimming-pool.

## *How to turn your swimming-pool into a trout hatchery*

Glittering like a semi-precious jewel in the golden light of an endless South African summer, a properly-maintained suburban swimming-pool can be your home's most sparkling liquid asset. All it takes is patience, discipline, and a store-room full of highly combustible chemicals that are probably past their expiry date because you still haven't figured out how to get the lid off.

It is for this reason that more and more pool-owning householders are turning to trout-farming for pleasure and profit. All you need is a medium-sized suburban swimming-pool that hasn't been cleaned, filtered, backwashed, or swum in for a few months, as well as two trout.

These are obtainable from the Eastern Transvaal. Put trout in pool and feed on leaves and other stuff in pool. Leave to simmer until hatched, and use net to net. Put sign outside house saying 'TROUT/FOREL', and sell to people who don't know how to get to Eastern Transvaal.

# *How To Have A Great Depression*
## *Managing your finances in South Africa today*

According to economists, financial experts, scenario planners, and the bloke falling off the barstool in the corner, South Africa is heading for its Greatest Depression since the West Indies beat us by 20 wickets with two balls to spare in Jamaica. Or was it 25 wickets?

Either way, the forthcoming Great Depression will be welcomed by South Africans of all creeds and colours, because it means that the Recession is finally over.

'Thank goodness for that,' says financial-planning guru Magnus Overdraft, whose daily, weekly, bi-monthly, and semi-annual advice columns are avidly read by people who can still afford to borrow someone else's newspaper.

'That must rank as one of the most mediocre recessions we have ever been through,' said Mr Overdraft, adding another notch to his cardboard belt with a ballpoint pen. 'But I must say, it definitely looks as if we are heading for a Great Depression.'

Here are some of the main trends, as outlined in a quarterly report by one of South Africa's most respected experts on the Depression, who may not be named because he is too depressing.

The money supply is expected to tighten dramatically towards the second half of the first quarter, and it will be almost impossible to find change for the parking meter. However, this situation will ease slightly when the Reserve Bank issues its new series of R10, R20, and R50 coins.

In order to save money, the coins will be manufactured from recycled aluminium cool-drink cans. This is likely to place renewed pressure on Precious Metals, and the price of an ounce of gold will reach a new psychological low of the price of 250 grams of margarine.

At the same time, the Consumer Price Index will reach a new psychological high of double what it was the day before, while psychologists' fees will reach a new psychological high of whatever you have in your pocket, as long as it's cash.

The good news is that inflation is likely to stabilise around the triple-figure mark, due to the fact that consumers will not have enough money to spend on anything worth inflating. There will be a slight upswing in the economy towards the third fourth of the fifth quarter, when the Minister of Finance is expected to announce his intention to return to full-time study in order to find out what a 'BA Rate' is.

Meanwhile, all indications are that the BA Rate will follow a firm course of contra-cyclical fluctuation before settling into a trough of depression, and that South Africa will beat New Zealand by 22 runs in the action replay of the Non-Racial Constituent Assembly Whites-Only Referendum Cricket Cup.

As these projections reveal, South Africans are going to have to keep a close watch on their finances as the economic spiral continues to plummet in a downward direction.

If you are too busy, it may be a good idea to hire an armed security guard to keep a close watch on your finances, along with a trained Rottweiler to keep a close watch on the security guard.

Meanwhile, here are the answers to some commonly asked questions about the Great Depression, and what you can do to maintain your equilibrium in the current economic climate.

*The other night, as I was busy filing my bills, accounts, letters of final demand and income tax assessment forms in the wastepaper basket, I heard the sounds of scratching and panting at my front door.*

*When I went to investigate, all I could see through the peephole were the iron bars of my security gate. Fortunately, I also have a peephole further down the door.*

*As I crouched to look through it, I found myself staring into the beady yellow eyes, menacing fangs, and slavering jaws of Wolf, my faithful pet Alsatian. Was I relieved! I had thought for a moment that it was a wolf at the door.*

*My question is, do you have any suggestions for keeping Wolf from the door, as he is ruining the paintwork with his constant scratching.*

As the bitter winds of the Great Depression begin biting into the tattered fabric of the South African economy, more and more householders across the country are battling to keep the wolf from the door.

However, there is no real cause for concern, as the wolf is not indigenous to South Africa, and is usually found only in the North American tundra and parts of the Arctic Circle.

Keeping debt collectors and deputy sheriffs from the door is another matter, however, and you are therefore advised to get yourself a large wolf.

*Looking through my pockets the other day, I found a small sum of money that had somehow escaped the attention of my wife. I would now like to invest part of this sum on the Stock Exchange, and was wondering if you could tell me whether I am likely to achieve a higher return by investing in 'Bulls', or 'Bears'.*

Putting your excess capital on the Stock Exchange is a risky proposition, but the rewards can be great for your stockbroker. To find yourself a stockbroker, simply stand outside the Stock Exchange Building and wave a blank cheque in the air.

The following brief glossary will help you understand what happens next. For further information, please consult your stockbroker.

*Stockbroker:* Person who sells you stock and leaves you broker than you were to begin with.

*Debentures:* What you get from your debentist after you've lost your teeth on the Stock Exchange.

*How to keep the wolf from your door.*

*Bullish:* What investment advisers are full of. 'I'm feeling very bullish today. Give me all your money, and I'll tell you what to do with it.'

*Bearish:* Typical behaviour of investor attempting to track down broker after Stock Exchange 'correction'.

*Correction:* What newspapers publish in small print at the bottom of page seven the day after running a front-page editorial slamming rumours that the Stock Exchange is about to collapse.

*Crash:* What happens when two stockbrokers are too busy talking on their car-phones to notice that the lights have changed.

*Junk Bonds:* Actors who have tried unsuccessfully to play the role of 007, following Sean Connery's retirement. George Lazenby and Timothy Dalton are perhaps the best-known 'Junk Bonds'.

*I have heard that it is possible to make a million rand with a once-only investment of R50. Is this true, and if so, where do I get the R50?*

Making your first million in a depressed economic climate is never easy, but it is also guaranteed to be an experience you will never forget. You will need to ask your bank manager for a R50 note, which he will gladly lend you on receipt of an item of equivalent worth, such as your car.

Now place the R50 note neatly on top of the glass, and put the lid of the colour copier firmly down to smooth out any creases. Punch in '20 000' where it says Number of Copies, and then press the green start button.

Make sure there is enough paper in the tray before you repeat the process with the other side of the note. It is always a good idea to run off an extra 500 000 or so, in case you are given the option of a fine.

*With the Great Depression looming, I have decided to follow the advice of my grocer and stock up on tinned foods, in order to make a fortune selling tinned foods to people who forgot to stock up on tinned foods before the Depression.*

*Could you please tell me which varieties of tinned food are likely to produce the greatest yield per capital expenditure in the medium to long term, and also which supermarket chain offers the lowest prices on a trolley-for-trolley basis.*

As you suggest, the outlook on tinned foods is very bullish at the moment, with particular emphasis on tinned bully-beef. With its high protein content and wide range of domestic and military applications, tinned bully-beef is regarded by many analysts as the 'Blue Chip' of tinned foods.

Should you find any blue chips in your tin of bully-beef, please return to manufacturer for a prompt and courteous refund. If you are serious about investing in the tinned food market, however, the important thing to remember is, 'don't put all your tins in one basket'. Rather use a trolley.

This will allow you to spread your portfolio across the broadest possible range of tinned foods, from Pilchards in Tomato Sauce to Baked Beans in Tomato Sauce to Spicy Meatballs in Tomato Sauce to Whole Peeled Tomatoes in Whole Peeled Tomato Sauce.

Other tempting propositions for the adventurous tinned food speculator include Pineapple Rings in Pineapple Juice, Cape Mussels in Port Wine Sauce, Spears of Asparagus in French Onion Sauce, and Aluminium Alloy Tins With The Labels Ripped Off By Some Bored Juvenile Delinquent Shopping With His Mother.

The nearest tinned food packer will be pleased to point you in the direction of these items as soon as he has finished slapping new barcode-stickers over the old barcode-

*The Great Tinned Food Crash of 1992.*

stickers. It is this practice of 'over-pricing' that makes the tinned food market such an attractive arena for the forward-thinking investor.

The best time to buy tinned foods is during a 'Gigantic Sale', when prices can plummet by up to 7,5 per cent as selected barcode-stickers are peeled off to make way for the next batch.

If you really want to take the tinned food market by storm, however, here's an insider tip guaranteed to take you all the way to the top of the pile. Buy tin-openers.

## *When The Going Gets Tough, The Tough Go Shopping*

From Eastgate to Westgate, from Northgate to Southgate, from Citygate to Villagegate to Inkathagate, shopping centres have become the vibrant heart and soul of South African community life. Whether you're looking for a security-gate, a driveway gate, or just a tube of Colgate, you're guaranteed to find it in a big shopping centre named after a gate.

Even if you're not looking for anything in particular, you're still guaranteed to find it, providing you remember to bring along a blank housekeeping cheque signed by your husband or reasonable facsimile thereof.

Research shows that up to 50 per cent of all people wandering around a shopping centre are not looking for anything in particular, while the remaining 50 per cent are desperately trying to locate a specific item, such as the white Toyota Conquest they could have sworn they parked on the

B level of the Pink block on the east side of Greatermans six hours ago. In the meantime, they may as well go shopping.

Psychologists refer to this mode of behaviour as 'spontaneous consumption', and many believe it can go a long way towards reducing stress caused by work and family pressures, high-density traffic situations, and final letters of demand from psychologists located in shopping centres.

Most South African shopping centres open their gates between 8 am and 6 pm every Monday, Tuesday, Wednesday, Thursday, Friday, and Saturday, but many are now also authorised to open on special occasions, such as Sunday. In terms of section 4 (i) of the Sunday Observance Act of 1910, however, merchants are obliged to shut their doors at 1 pm on a Sunday, in order to allow members of the public to attend the 2 pm screening of *American Ninja 6* on the mezzanine level.

Of course, there is much more to going shopping than going shopping, going to the movies, going shopping, going to the bank, going shopping, going to get your hair done, going shopping, going to lunch, going shopping, going to get your legs waxed, going shopping, and going shopping.

To begin with, there is parking.

## *Parking*

Before the invention of the decentralised multi-level regional shopping complex in 1972, people who were driven by an inexplicable compulsion to rush out and buy things had no obligation but to battle noxious exhaust fumes and foul-mouthed fellow motorists *en route* to the central business district of the nearest 'big city'.

Once there, they were forced to spend hours looking for a

vacant parking bay, minutes looking for change in the correct combination of denominations, and seconds actually doing the month's shopping before running back to collect the pink ticket and kick the left front tyre.

Today, with shopping centres conveniently located near the off-ramps of the major inter-suburban freeway networks, getting there is half the fun, and finding somewhere to park when you get there is the other half.

Parking-space is a major priority in the architectural design of the contemporary suburban shopping centre, and you are guaranteed to find a vacant bay within 950m of the big brown sub-building with the auxiliary power-plant and the plumbing for the piped music. Well, you are welcome to it. The rest of us will try our luck on the roundabout.

According to research conducted by people who have nothing better to do than drive around and around the main entrance of a big suburban shopping centre, driving around and around the main entrance of a big suburban shopping centre is one of the most effective ways of securing a parking-space that will save you having to walk 200m to the main entrance before you walk 15,6km around the shopping centre.

However, certain procedures and formalities should be observed while on the roundabout, in order to ensure that all shoppers have a fair and equal chance of stealing someone else's parking-space. To begin with, the recommended speed limit on the roundabout is 8 km/h, unless you have just seen an old lady reversing out of a parking-space, in which case you may accelerate to 120 km/h before the old lady decides to switch off her engine and go back to Woolworths to exchange her medium pantihose for a large.

As a matter of courtesy, you should wait until a person has

*South African shopper patiently waiting for prime parking-space outside main entrance of shopping centre.*

completely pulled out of a parking-space before you attempt to pull in. Many people are reluctant to abandon a Grade A parking-space simply because they have finished shopping for the day, and the sight of frantic drivers competing for the spot is only likely to make them get out and catch the bus home instead.

Please remember that any parking bay marked 'FIRE', 'AMBULANCE', 'LOADING-ZONE', or 'POLICE' is strictly reserved for any person who gets there before you do.

Should a dispute arise over the right to occupy a bona fide empty parking-space, an independent mediator may be called in to occupy the space while the parties repeatedly ram each other's bumpers with their 4 x 4's. In the meantime, the mediator may want to go off and do some shopping.

## *How to find your way around a big suburban shopping centre*

Once you have found a safe and convenient spot to park your car, and you have made sure that the windows are closed and the doors are locked, the next vital step is to run around looking for a security guard who will be able to stick a wire-hanger through the side-window and remove your car-keys from the ignition.

If you are unable to find a security guard, don't let it worry you too much, unless you have also parked your car on a downhill with the handbrake off and the ignition on. The important thing is, you are now ready to go shopping.

Before you step into the shopping centre itself, however, you will be required to walk through an 'infra-red' security screening device just outside the main entrance. Do not be alarmed.

The purpose of the device is to determine whether you are carrying any metallic objects on your person, such as forks, keys, belt-buckles, hairclips, ear-rings, television aerials, stainless-steel mixing-bowls, R2 coins, solid silver Sheffield sugar-bowls stolen from the Blue Train, and infra-red shopping centre security screening devices.

In the unlikely event that you do not have any metallic objects on your person, you will be given an opportunity to go and fetch a hub-cap from your car. Then you may try again. It is not customary to tip the security guard on such occasions.

Once you have breached the portals of the shopping centre, you will need to consult a map in order to determine where you are. Maps are located at strategic intersections in most of the major shopping centres, so your first priority will be to locate a strategic intersection. Please consult your nearest map.

Here you will find an arrow pointing to a big white dot, along with a message confirming that 'You Are Here'. If you would actually prefer to be somewhere else, it is best to remember that shopping centres are generally divided into three separate areas: U (Upper), M (Mezzanine), and L (Lost).

To find your way from one level to another, all you have to do is enquire at the Information Counter of the nearest Big Store or Speciality Boutique. The lady behind the counter will be only too happy to point you in the direction of the Credit Application Department, following which you will be able to spend a few very satisfying hours buying things you don't need with money you don't have.

But don't be all day, because there are plenty of other

shops that would like to give you credit for not carrying any money on your person.

## *How to buy things you don't need with money you don't have*

Before the invention of Unlimited Credit Facilities and the Revolving Overdraft, people who did not have large wads of paper money in their pockets were generally restricted to window-shopping. Even then, according to one top window-shopper, the price of a small frosted bathroom window would be enough to shatter your housekeeping budget for the month.

But today, such discriminatory practices are a thing of the past, and even if you do not have a single R200 note in your possession, you will be able to stroll home with the finest double-door French Window patio-set in your shopping trolley. Please remember to return the trolley with your first payment.

If the payment will not fit in the trolley, you may telephone the Customer Relations Department, and they will be happy to send a forklift-driver and a former professional boxer around on the first of the month.

This method of shopping is known as 'having an account', and it is becoming increasingly popular with people who have already used up the budget facility on their credit cards. Contrary to popular belief, today's major department stores are becoming very strict and selective in deciding whether or not to allow someone to open an account.

The applicant will have to satisfy a stringent set of qualifications and requirements, such as being able to fill in a credit application form, and being present in the shop when the winner of the mystery one-and-a-half per cent discount for new account-holders is announced over the Public Address system at 11 o'clock on a Saturday morning.

There are many other advantages to being an account-holder at one or more of the major department stores. For instance, you will be entitled to take things home on 'appro' before you decide whether you would like to buy them or not.

'Appro' is short for 'Appropriation', meaning 'to take possession of before returning as unsuitable, but thanks anyway'. This facility can come in very handy if you are planning a major social event, in which case you might want to take 15 strapless satin cocktail gowns, 12 strapless velveteen tuxedos with matching sash and whatever a cummerbund is supposed to be, a black leather gomma-gomma lounge suite with zebra-fur scatter cushions, some pot-plants, 200 packets of kettle-fried crisps, a domestic servant's uniform, and four crates of French Champagne before deciding that they were unfortunately the wrong size, but thanks anyway.

Another very practical reason for opening an account is the fact that you will be sent a free account-holder's magazine every month, unless you have not paid your account, in which case you will be sent two free account-holder's magazines.

You will also be entitled to a wide range of Limited Special Offers, such as 'Pay Your Account Within Ninety Days Or We Call Jimmy Abbott', and you will no longer have to face the disheartening prospect of driving all the way out to your Post Office box to discover that no one has sent you a letter.

But perhaps most importantly, having an account means never having to say you have nothing to do on a Saturday morning, or for that matter, a Sunday, Monday, Tuesday, Wednesday, Thursday, Friday, or Saturday afternoon.

## *What to do about Compulsive Shopping Syndrome (CSS)*

Mrs X (not her real name) is a typical 29-year-old professional woman residing somewhere in the north-western suburbs of Johannesburg (not her real address).

Until a few months ago, this stylish, attractive blonde (not her real hairdo) earned a lucrative six-figure salary as the chief clothes-buyer for a major retail concern (not her real job).

But today, Mrs X is one of a growing number of 29-year-old professional women who have fallen victim to the harrowing acronym known as CSS. Compulsive Shopping Syndrome. Mrs X agreed to speak about her experiences of this gruelling condition on the strict condition that it did not take all day, as she had a lot of shopping to do before going shopping.

Standing near the back of the brunchtime queue at Stefanie's in Hyde Park, Mrs X confessed that she was close to breaking-point, and did not think she would be able to take it for very much longer.

'I don't think I can take it for very much longer,' she said. 'We've been standing in this queue for two-and-a-half hours, and we haven't moved an inch! And those people at that table over there haven't even touched their Waldorf Salad. Can't they see we're waiting?'

Picking up her 15 shopping-bags with a heavy sigh, Mrs X moved forward an inch and began to recount her nightmarish story.

*How to recognise a person with Compulsive Shopping Syndrome (CSS).*

'Just hang on a second,' she said. 'I first want to re-count my shopping-bags. Ten, twelve, fourteen ... oh, no! Someone's stolen my small Woolworths' bag! Quick, call the security guar ... oh. Here it is in my big Stuttafords' bag. Hmmm. I wonder if they've got Tuna Mayonnaise on the menu today. That's what they had yesterday, and I had to ask the waiter for a serviette to wipe it off so I could see what was on the menu. Here, you hold on to these shopping-bags. I'm going to see whether there's anything on sale at Garlick's. And don't lose my place in the queue.'

Three hours later, Mrs X returned to take up her place in what was now the lunchtime queue at Stefanie's. Although there had been nothing on sale at Garlick's, Mrs X was laden down with parcels from Dodo's, where she had gone to overcome a bout of depression brought on by the fact that there was nothing on sale at Garlick's.

Suddenly, the waiter clicked his fingers and led us to a small table in the corner. Glancing at his watch, he said we should not have to wait more than two hours for chairs, although knives and forks would take a little longer. In the meantime, Mrs X decided that she may as well go over to Woolworths to exchange the black-and-white stirrup-leg ski-pants she had bought this morning for a white-and-black pair.

'I can't help myself,' she explained. 'Whenever I cross the threshold of a shop, my pulse starts racing and I feel driven by an inexplicable urge to dispose of my husband's income, following which I am gripped by tidal waves of guilt and despair that can only be conquered by going shopping. Bye. Oh, and please order me a double Perrier with lots of ice made out of ordinary tap-water, and have it sent up to the second fitting-room from the left in Lingerie.'

According to a psychologist who may not be named for

reasons of having just been made up, Compulsive Shopping Syndrome (CSS) is nothing to worry about, and can easily be treated by asking your bank manager for an overdraft on your overdraft. Bye.

## *Follow That Minibus!*
### *How to hijack-proof your vehicle*

If you are the registered owner of a 16-seater station-wagon, 14-seater pick-up truck, 20-seater four-wheel-drive, 50-seater armoured car, or 220-seater furniture delivery van with lounge suites in the back, you are advised to take the following precautions in order to prevent your vehicle from being converted for use as a licensed minibus taxi without your express written permission.

According to a spokesman for the Minibus Liberation Movement (MLM), the most foolproof method is to give your express written permission. The recommended format is:

'I, the undersigned, being the registered owner of a vehicle that would make a nice minibus, do hereby declare that I am no longer the registered owner of a vehicle that would make a nice minibus.

I furthermore declare that the aforesaid vehicle is free of any major mechanical flaws or defects, although these can always be added at a later stage. To the best of my knowledge, there are no outstanding traffic fines to be paid on this vehicle, unless of course you really want to pay them.

In good faith, and without prejudice to my statutory

rights, I therefore now hand over the keys to this vehicle for use at the sole discretion of the person standing opposite me with the full-face balaclava and the cultural weapon.

Yours Sincerely, the Undersigned.'

You will then be handed a Change of Ownership Form for insurance purposes, following which you will be conveyed to the destination of your choice for a nominal fee. It is customary on occasions such as these to give the driver a small tip, such as your wallet.

Make sure that you remove your insurance broker's business-card beforehand.

Comprehensive insurance policies for vehicles that would make a nice minibus are available for not much more than the estimated replacement cost of the vehicle, plus a small administrative charge.

It is possible, however, to reduce this figure by up to 2,5 per cent if you take the following additional measures:

1. Camouflage. Research in the field has shown that vehicles that would make a nice minibus are five times less likely to be liberated if they are painted in camouflage colours and hidden in a field.

Two-tone camouflage paint in a variety of shades is available from your nearest military surplus store. Apply liberally, and cover with twigs, leaves, bits of grass, and empty beer-cartons.

Park vehicle in field, and catch minibus taxi to and from work. If you are unable to locate your vehicle on your return, please contact your insurance broker.

2. Painting your registration number on the roof of your vehicle. Aside from giving skydivers something to read while waiting for their parachutes to open, this simple precaution will make it much easier for your vehicle to be

traced in the event of its liberation.

Don't forget to ask your insurance broker for your complimentary 'IF YOU CAN READ THE NUMBER-PLATE ON MY ROOF, YOU'RE TOO DARN CLOSE' bumper-sticker.

3. Stencil a warning message to would-be hijackers on the back of your vehicle. Something along the lines of 'Warning, This Vehicle Is Under 24-Hour Armed Surveillance By A Highly-Trained Private Security Firm' should suffice.

While this is unlikely to deter a determined would-be hijacker, it will at least provide you with the opportunity to jump back into the driver's seat and roar away while your would-be hijacker reads the notice and collapses with laughter on the tarmac.

4. Equip your vehicle with a car telephone. Should your vehicle be liberated, you will then be able to telephone your hijacker from the nearest call-box and leave a rude message on the answering machine.

5. Fit your vehicle with a sophisticated electronic tracking device. This system has been successfully tested in the Kruger National Park, where elephants and other heavy-duty animals are sometimes made to wear radio-controlled bracelets around their ankles.

The animals can then easily be tracked from a central control-room if they do not come home in time for supper. To date, very few cases of elephant-hijacking have been reported, so you may want to apply for permission to convey some elephants in your trunk when you next go out shopping in your station-wagon.

6. Use the Porsche.

Aside from these recommendations, you are also advised to

*Anti-hijack system recommended by nine out of ten leading South African insurance companies.*

exercise extreme caution when slowing down or stopping at a traffic intersection, lay-by, yield sign, freeway off-ramp, loading zone, speed-bump, speed-trap, roadblock, toll-booth, minibus taxi rank, or designated vehicle liberation area.

Do not wind down your window if anyone approaches you with a complimentary advertising pamphlet while your car is in a stationary position, unless you are satisfied that the pamphlet contains a bona fide discount offer on electronic in-car security systems.

## *How To Defect To The African National Congress*

Unemployed Security Policemen, disillusioned Democratic Party Members of Parliament, Afrikaner Weerstandsbeweging horsemen who can't find their way out of Mamelodi, and Pan Africanist Congress members who have temporarily run out of bullets.

These are just some of the people who have recently applied for asylum in the ranks of the African National Congress, an organisation open to anyone who is committed to peace, democracy, and some sort of job in the Civil Service.

However, there are certain conditions.

While the Internal Exiles Wing of the African National Congress welcomes genuine enquiries from all South Africans, irrespective of race, sex, creed, or incorrect political affiliation, right of admission is strictly reserved for security reasons.

If you are a security reason, therefore, you may want to complete the following application form and psychometric questionnaire and post it to your nearest divisional branch of the African National Congress.

On second thoughts, as the Post Office is scheduled to be on strike until further notice, would you please rather hand it to your nearest retrenched Security Policeman, and he can drop it off at our next meeting.

TO WHOM IT MAY CONCERN

I (name, rank, number) hereby wish to apply for membership of the African National Congress, an organisation I have admired and supported ever since I can remember. My current political affiliation is (please tick one only):
▫ Card-carrying Nationalist
▫ Credit-card-carrying Socialist
▫ Reincarnated National Socialist
▫ Licensed Anarchist
▫ Unlicensed Television-Viewer
▫ Used to be top-ranking member of African National Congress, until unmasked as Security Police spy at annual Security Policemen's Masked Ball
▫ Sorry, I don't remember

While we are on the subject, I would like to use this opportunity to unconditionally renounce any uninformed and misguided opinions I may or not have held on the ANC in the distant past, and I would also like to apologise unreservedly for the glaring split infinitive in the second clause of this sentence.

In support of my application for full or associate

membership of your organisation, I attach hereunder a selection of qualifications and/or achievements from my curriculum vitae (please tick relevant qualifications and/or achievements):

▫ Can spell 'curriculum' without having to look up in dictionary
▫ Have Master's Degree in Political Philosophy
▫ Have Servant's Degree in Domestic Science
▫ Have no experience whatsoever in operating switchboard
▫ Did some freelance work in Social Welfare once
▫ Can ride horse (short distances only)
▫ Fluent in both official languages
▫ Understand a little English and Afrikaans too

Should my application be approved, I hereby agree to participate fully and openly in any 'de-briefing sessions' I may be required to attend. I do not foresee a problem in this area, as long as all the other participants are also required to remove their briefs.

Please note that this application is to be treated as strictly private and confidential, and that it is made without prejudice to my right to change my mind in the event that some other bunch gets into power.

Yours sincerely,

(Name and signature)

PS: If you need a character reference, please feel free to contact John Bishop at the SABC (I bumped into him at a supermarket once).

# *The Unrehabilitated Optimist's Guide To Codesa*
## *(Just in case. You never know)*

*Everywhere I go, I hear people talking about 'Codesa'. It's 'Codesa' this, 'Codesa' that, 'Codesa' the other. Please could you tell me what 'Codesa' stands for, and whether or not it is contagious.*

You are quite right. More and more people are going around talking about Codesa these days, and less and less people actually seem to have any idea what they are talking about. Yet the whole thing is very easily explained.

Codesa, which stands for 'Convention for delaying the transition to a democratic South Africa', is a multi-partisan negotiating forum that gets together every now and again in a sincere and concerted bid to determine whether there is any point in getting together ever again.

Once that has been sorted out, Codesa also takes a look at some crucial issues affecting the future of all South Africans, such as 'Should We Give The Rightwing A Small Boerestaat In The Karoo', 'Who Can We Get To Be Minister Of Finance In The Interim Government', and 'What Time Do We Break for Lunch'.

In answer to your second question, there is no firm evidence as yet to suggest that Codesa is contagious. However, independent researchers claim to have established a link between attendance at Codesa and a range of short-term psychosomatic conditions, including delusion, depression, confusion, and falling asleep on the table during speeches by Zac de Beer.

If you are concerned about catching anything from

Codesa, you are best advised to join one of several concerned citizens' organisations, such as the Azanian People's Organisation or the Afrikaner Weerstandsbeweging. Also, try to keep away from Kempton Park.

*Kempton Park? What's Kempton Park got to do with it?*

As the official venue for Codesa's on-and-off-going Constitutional deliberations, the historic Transvaal metropolis of Kempton Park is perhaps best known for the fact that it is located right next door to the control tower at Jan Smuts Airport.

For the proud residents of quaint and colourful 'Kempton', as it is affectionately known, living with the constant whining and screaming of jet engines is a small price to pay for the privilege of living with the constant whining and screaming of delegates to Codesa.

So important has Codesa become to Kempton Park's social, economic, and cultural life, that the city council has applied to have the convention's head office at the World Trade Centre turned into a national monument.

'Before Codesa moved in here,' said a spokesman, 'this building could only be described as a White Elephant. Today, it can only be described as a Non-Racial Elephant. If there is anyone in the world who would like to come and trade here, they are more than welcome.'

*OK, so who are these people who go to Codesa, and what do they actually do all day long?*

Delegates to Codesa are drawn from the ranks of some of South Africa's top political parties and organisations, ranging from 'The Government' to 'The Next Government' to 'People Who Haven't Got A Hope Of Being In The Government Either Way, But Are Basically

Too Polite To Turn Down An Invitation To Negotiate Themselves Out Of Power'.

Each party or organisation is entitled to send as many delegates, attorneys, aides, stenographers, under-secretaries and plainclothes security personnel as may be deemed necessary to intimidate other parties and organisations, although a limit of 42 per delegation is generally applied for catering purposes.

Delegates who bring their own sandwiches are excluded from this total.

To answer the second part of your question, here is a comprehensive breakdown of an average delegate's working day at Codesa:

*7.30 am:* Arrive at World Trade Centre, Kempton Park. Valet parking available for members of National Party delegation. All other delegations must please remember to delegate one delegate to run outside and feed parking meter on hourly basis.

*8.15 am:* Working breakfast, including last-minute revisions to amended agenda for inter-delegational plenary sessions, secondary proofreading of preliminary draft of preamble to Constitution, and updating of opening addresses to full sitting of Codesa.

*9.45 am:* Brief recess to allow removal of egg, marmalade, and coffee stains from aforementioned documents and neckties.

*10.30 am:* Official opening of current Codesa session by neutral chairperson or other invited speaker with no affiliation to any political party or organisation represented at Codesa. Today's address will be delivered by Eugene Terre'Blanche of the AWB.

*12.15 pm:* Tea and sandwiches. Choice of white, brown, wholewheat, rye, pumpernickel, and garlic. Please remember that these will be available on a first come, first served basis, and that delegates at the back of the queue will have no option but to eat cake.

*1 pm for 1.30 pm:* Buffet luncheon. Mingling optional. The Catering Sub-Committee of Codesa regrets that custard pies will no longer be available on the dessert table, following an incident involving several hundred delegates at Codesa 2.

*3.15 pm:* Break for work.

*3.30 pm:* Afternoon tea with rusks.

*5.15 pm:* Take seats in main conference hall for speech on Constitutional Federalism by Amichand Rajbansi of the National People's Party.

*7.45 pm:* Pack up belongings and leave main conference hall, unless you are Amichand Rajbansi of the National People's Party.

*8.00 pm:* Pay parking fine at nearest police station. Go home.

*It all sounds very interesting. How do I go about getting a ticket to attend some of the sessions, and will there be any objection if I bring along a good book to read?*

Unfortunately, all opening and closing sessions of Codesa are closed to all members of the public, with the exception of bona fide accredited media representatives who have brought along a good book to read.

All Working Group, Plenary, and Management Committee sessions are also closed to all members of the public, with the exception of bona fide accredited tea-ladies who have brought along a nice tray of sandwiches.

It is felt by the Public Relations Advisory Committee of Codesa that the presence of media or members of the public at such sessions would tend to inhibit the frank and fruitful interchange of demands and accusations, as well as yawning, chain-smoking, and picking one's nose.

If you would like to attend such a session, therefore, you may wish to apply for a position as a tea-lady at Codesa.

*These 'Working Groups'. Could you briefly explain their role and function at Codesa, and also, what do they do when they're not working?*

Codesa's Working Groups, so-called to distinguish themselves from Not Really Working Groups, Generic Pin-Striped Suits Groups, and Just Standing Around The Sandwich Tray Waiting For Someone To Tell Us What To Do Groups, are small, secret groups of hand-picked delegates from across the South African political spectrum.

They meet behind closed doors, bolted windows, and sealed air-vents in a Restricted Access section of the World Trade Centre's nuclear fallout shelter (Mezzanine Level), and can be identified only by their secret handshake: a scowl, a glare, and an icy refusal to shake hands.

There are five Codesa Working Groups, and each is entrusted with a particular area of urgent national concern. These are as follows:

*Working Group One:* Creating A Favourable Climate For Democracy, Or At Least Getting Someone In To Take A Look At The Air-conditioning;

*Working Group Two:* Drawing Up A Democratic Constitution, Without Making It Look As If We Copied The Whole Thing From The Americans;

*Working Group Three:* Taking Care Of All The Nagging Little Details For The Transition To A Non-Racial Democratic State, Such As Our Pensions;

*Working Group Four:* Looking At The Future Of Transkei, Bophuthatswana, Venda, and Ciskei, Now That

Everyone Is Allowed To Play Blackjack In Seapoint;

*Working Group Five:* Looking For Electronic Listening Devices in the Cheese and Marmite Sandwiches.

I trust this answers both parts of your question.

*Being a delegate at Codesa sounds like a tough and very stressful assignment. What recreational and other facilities are available for delegates at the World Trade Centre?*

As you correctly assume, negotiating a brighter future for all South Africans is not a task for the faint-hearted. With this in mind, the conveners of Codesa have ensured that a wide range of facilities is available for anyone who wishes to build up energy or let off steam.

Before the day's proceedings get under way, delegates are encouraged to refine their strong-arm tactics with a pulse-quickening workout in Codesa's fully-equipped gymnasium, where the ultimate challenge is lifting a bound copy of *The Collected Speeches of Amichand Rajbansi* off the floor and holding it above your head for 30 seconds. So far, only Amichand Rajbansi has been able to do this.

Alternatively, delegates may want to sign up for expert courses in Kung-Fu, Ju-Jitsu, and Kickboxing, although these are only available to bona fide signatories of the National Peace Accord. For the less energetic, a few hours in a swirling jacuzzi or steam bath soothes aching muscles and offers a rare opportunity to escape the constant feeling that South Africa is slowly sinking in a giant tub of hot water.

Delegates who feel that they 'just need someone to talk to' after a hard day's deadlock, may want to lock themselves in one of Codesa's luxury 'Multi-Partisan Conversation Cubicles'. These are equipped with fully-stocked minibar, direct-dial telephone, and full directory of 087 advice lines.

There is no time limit on such calls, as all charges are automatically re-routed by Telkom's central computer to selected householders in the PWV triangle.

Finally, all delegates have unlimited access to Codesa's 'Fun and Games' room, where the choice of activities ranges from chess to snooker to pinball to watching slow-motion video replays of Eugene Terre'Blanche falling off his horse.

*Why are there so few female delegates at Codesa, and what is being done to remedy this glaring imbalance?*

It is certainly true that women are conspicuous by their absence in the halls, corridors, canteens, boardrooms and chambers of Codesa's headquarters at the World Trade Centre in Kempton Park.

The reason can be traced to a chauvinistic, outmoded, and ideologically incorrect policy decision in terms of which delegates to Codesa are not allowed to bring their wives.

This is due to 'limited catering facilities and the fact that having too many women around the place would tend to inhibit the frank and fruitful interchange of rude jokes at lunchtime,' explained a spokesman.

However, the policy is currently being reviewed by a special sub-committee as the result of a formal submission by a group of concerned South African women who were not invited to Codesa. The special sub-committee consists of 17 men, although the tea-lady is allowed in every now and again.

*OK, so what happens after Codesa?*

Nothing much. Usually, delegates just go out for a couple of quick toots at a nearby one-star hotel. But if it's been a really long day, they'll probably tend to wait until they get home.

*No, what I actually meant to say was, what happens to all of us in South Africa, once Codesa has fulfilled its role?*

Oh. Well, let's put it this way. The road to Codesa has been a difficult and hazardous one, strewn with obstacles and lined with seemingly insurmountable barriers to open, effective communication between diametrically opposing political parties and organisations.

Codesa has been able to prove that it is possible for at least some of those parties and organisations to come together at least some of the time in a bid to resolve at least some of their differences.

If we look beyond Codesa, we will see that the road, long and winding as it may be, leads almost directly to the international departure lounge at Jan Smuts Airport. Don't worry. We're doing our best to find a shortcut.


## *How To Barricade Your Suburb*

Thanks to the abolition of such outdated discriminatory laws as the Group Areas Act and the Land Act, it has become possible for South Africans of all creeds and colours to coexist as neighbours in the dusty, sprawling townships of their choice.

Despite this newfound freedom, more and more people are opting to stay in the suburbs, where the air is clean, the nights are quiet, and the panoramic vista of the rugged koppies across the veld is interrupted only by the dazzling glint of sunlight on the corrugated-iron roofs of the informal settlements.

It is in quiet, reflective moments such as these, that

formal settlers may feel compelled to cast aside petty political differences and extend the hand of friendship across their high security walls and in-built cultural barriers. For it is only by standing together, shoulder-to-shoulder, that residents of these peaceful and democratic communities will be able to convince informal settlers that they are more than welcome to settle in someone else's backyard.

If you are the kind of person who believes that all South Africans should enjoy an equal opportunity to pay rates, taxes, and the interest on their outstanding bond repayments, you may want to resort to the following plan of decentralised mass action.

If not, don't worry too much. The neighbours will handle it.

## *What to do in the event of an impending informal resettlement*

When an established suburban community finds itself on the verge of being informally resettled, it is vital that residents remain calm and respond to the situation with extreme sensitivity and tact.

Should you see evidence of informal settlers in the vicinity of your neighbourhood, all you need to do is discreetly press your panic button three or four times, and then go back to whatever you were doing before you ran through the house trying to remember where you left your panic button.

Since panic button batteries have a tendency to fail when under pressure, however, you may want to telephone the Flying Squad and ask them to press their own panic buttons as a backup measure.

Also, if you have a Citizen Force commando unit in your area, there can be no harm in asking them to send around any citizens who may have reported for duty and would now like something to do. A task force of trained negotiators will be on the scene within minutes, and you will be able to watch them through binoculars after pointing them in the right direction.

Remember to stay indoors, as the rotors of descending Police and Army helicopters can whip up dust-storms that may prove irritating to sensitive eyes.

It is also a good idea to keep your own attack dogs inside the yard, in order to prevent them from attacking other attack dogs who are only trying to do their duty.

Be sure to demand proper identification from any uniformed security personnel who may knock on your door to inform you that they have found the small piece of corrugated iron that you dumped in the veld a few days earlier because it wouldn't fit in your dustbin when you remodelled your garden shed.

The point is, you can never be too careful.

## *How to elect a neighbourhood representative who will be able to decide what to do next*

From time to time, according to guidelines drawn up by people who draw up guidelines from time to time, designated Government or Provincial authorities may decide to designate certain areas of land as 'Designated Informal Settlement Areas'.

This is part of an ongoing campaign by the South African Government to redress historical imbalances of land distribution, and is nothing to worry about if you do not live across the road from a Designated Informal Settlement Area.

To find out if any such areas are due to be proclaimed in your immediate neighbourhood, please consult the full-colour property section of this week's bumper-issue *Government Gazette*, which also features a mouth-watering potjiekos recipe, step-by-step instructions on how to crochet an attractive two-tone cover for your panic button, and details of an exciting Finders Keepers competition in which you can win one of seven fragments of Bophuthatswana.

You will find the Designated Informal Settlement Area listings on the first 15 pages of the property section, just before 'Cabinet Ministers' Residences For Sale'.

Should an area of open veld, grassland, swamp, marsh, bog, mire, moor, meadow, pasture, public park or rugby-field in the vicinity of your home be listed as a Designated Informal Settlement Area, you will generally have the right to lodge an appeal within 15 (fifteen) days from date of publication. But you will have to move quickly.

Circle the relevant listing in bold red ink, underline several times, surround with arrows, exclamation marks, and stickers marked 'Urgent', and lodge between security grilles of neighbour's front door when Rottweiler is inside having supper.

Your neighbour will then spring into action, and within 14 (fourteen) days, you will find the following note lodged between your Dobermann Pinscher's teeth:

## URGENT URGENT URGENT!

Dear Neighbour,

Allow me to introduce myself. I am your neighbour. Although we have not actually met, you have probably seen me on weekends, fixing my roof, washing my car, painting my wall, cleaning my pool, mowing my lawn, and generally maintaining my property and surroundings for the benefit of the community at large.

It is with this in mind that I have decided to call a 'Mass Meeting of Neighbours' in order to discuss the impending proclamation of a Designated Informal Settlement Area in the open plot of land across the road from the disused electrical sub-station next to the corrugated iron and cardboard recycling depot.

I am sure you will agree that, inasmuch as we have always been willing to welcome new neighbours to our neighbourhood, this arbitrary and authoritarian rezoning of valuable land is likely to prove detrimental to property prices and our view of the disused electrical sub-station next to the corrugated iron and cardboard recycling depot.

Since I am currently in the process of recarpeting the master bathroom and installing razor-wire in the ceiling, I was wondering if we could possibly all meet at your place around 7 pm for 7.30 pm.

I will bring the potato salad and the blazing kerosene torches. The bloke across the road has promised to see if he can dig up some spare pitchforks. I usually drink Black Label, but if you have cold Hansa, that's also OK.

Yours in the spirit of good neighbourliness,

Your Neighbour

PS: I can recommend someone who will be able to take a look at some of the bigger cracks in your garden wall, if you're interested.

## *How to reach an informal settlement, and what to do if that doesn't work*

Before you and your neighbours embark on any plan of mass protest action, it is vital that you exhaust every possible avenue of negotiation in an attempt to reach an informal settlement.

To do this, get hold of a map of your neighbourhood and drive down every avenue until you feel exhausted. If you come across a person loitering with intent at a four-way stop street, wind your window down a few millimetres and ask if they would mind pointing you in the general direction of the nearest informal settlement.

This might also be a good opportunity to reach into your cubby-hole for a can of black spray-paint. Give it a thorough shake, and hand to the person with instructions to spray 'INFORMAL SETTLEMENTS' in a neat scrawl beneath the big word on the stop sign.

Then it's off to the nearest informal settlement for a frank and fruitful discussion on ways to stop informal settlements. Through a careful combination of diplomacy, understanding, and open-minded, two-way communication, it should be possible to resolve the crisis in your neighbourhood without resorting to threats and confrontation.

But if your neighbours don't want to come along, you may have no other option.

It is best to travel in convoy, preferably in a hard-body

4 x 4 with wire-mesh welded to the windowframes in case of inclement weather.

Make sure that the windscreen-wipers are placed underneath the wire-mesh, or they may get damaged by loose pebbles churned up from the gravel by the rapidly accelerating wheels of the 4 x 4 in front. Before slamming the gear-lever into first and accelerating, please check that your Rottweiler is wearing his safety-belt.

Remember to maintain your minimum following distance at all times, unless you are driving the 4 x 4 in front. As you approach the perimeter of the informal settlement, slow down to cruising speed and reach for your 240 watt portable loudhailer with power-boosted internal speaker and built-in echo. Built-in echo.

With one elbow on the steering-wheel, put the loudhailer to your mouth and say something informal, such as 'Hello, hello . . . testing, testing . . . you have three-and-a-half minutes to disperse . . . all right then, make it four . . . hello, hello . . . can you hear me at the back . . . testing, 1, 2, 3 . . .'

Now try it again, this time with batteries in the loudhailer and the power-switch set to 'on'. On second thoughts, there's no point drawing unnecessary attention to yourself.

So put on the fog lights, grind the four-wheel drive, blow the fog-horn, and hurry back home to begin setting up the barricades.

## *Where to get hold of suburban barricades, and how to put them up*

According to the *South African Handbook of Suburban Guerrilla Warfare*, a 'barricade' is any large object or collection of objects designed to prevent unauthorised

*Formal settler protesting against impending informal settlement.*

access to the nicer parts of a suburb.

Suburban barricades are available in kit-form from your nearest reputable hardware store, but it is often more cost-effective to assemble your own from the following list of components: big, rusty oil-drums, with or without serrated lids; pre-cast concrete fence-slabs, with or without steel-reinforced posts; retreaded tyres, with or without retired treads; bricks; half-bricks; rocks; half-rocks; unserviceable washing-machines and/or tumble-driers; out-of-style television sets and/or video recorders covered by comprehensive insurance; sheets of corrugated cardboard; sheets of corrugated iron; corrugated sheets that are too difficult to iron; portable braais; potjiekos pots; porcelain statues of Rottweilers received as wedding gifts; tin bath-tubs to put the booze in; booze; and neighbours.

If you are unable to locate any of these items in your own backyard, try asking around at your nearest informal settlement. This may also be a good place to ask for volunteers to help you erect the barricades.

Choose a spot equidistant from the outskirts of your garden suburb and the inskirts of the informal settlement, and begin laying the barricades across a road that is relatively free of traffic.

Remember to allow access for emergency vehicles, such as bottle-store delivery-vans and outside-broadcast trucks from the SABC. At this point, it will be necessary to elect a neighbourhood spokesperson to deliver statements, answer probing questions from media representatives, and wave at friends and relatives who may be watching at home.

Be sure to elect a person who is able to articulate the legitimate grievances of your community in a reasoned, eloquent, charismatic yet conciliatory manner while wearing a full-face balaclava for professional reasons.

Here are some things you may want to say when the lady with the microphone asks why you are standing in the middle of a public thoroughfare surrounded by piles of builders' rubble and neighbours waving kerosene torches and uprooted stop signs in the air:

* 'We want to keep our neighbourhood tidy.'
* 'We fully understand the plight of the informal settlers, and are committed to finding them better accommodation in someone else's suburb.'
* 'There's nothing on TV.'
* 'As long-standing residents of this suburb, we are concerned that we will be unable to sell our houses when our emigration visas come through.'
* 'We're not racists, but we're always willing to learn.'
* 'I'd just like to say hi to all my friends and relatives who might be watching at home. Hi.'
* 'We demand an action replay of the Referendum.'
* 'Ag, it's always nice to get out and meet your neighbours.'
* 'Hey! I've suddenly remembered that I forgot to switch the alarm on before coming out to man the barricades!'

At this point, the informal protest will be formally abandoned in order to give everyone a chance to rush home and check the status of their alarms.

After the stresses and tensions of the day, it may also be a good idea for all participants to retire to bed early, secure in the knowledge that the barricades and obstacles will have been cleared by sunrise, and the road to a brighter future will once again be open to all law-abiding South Africans who would like to buy a cheap house in the area.

# Ten Great South African Inventions That Changed The World

*1. THE AUTOMATIC VACUUM-OPERATED SWIMMING-POOL CLEANER.* Before the invention of the automatic vacuum-operated swimming-pool cleaner in Boksburg in 1972, cleaning a swimming-pool was an arduous, time-consuming chore that often required the use of a fully equipped scuba-suit and lead-weighted underwater broom by the domestic servant delegated to clean the pool.

As a result, it became almost impossible to find domestic servants who would do pools. It was with this in mind that a South African inventor of automatic vacuum-operated swimming-pool cleaning devices began inventing the simple yet revolutionary device that would allow domestic servants to get on with more important tasks, such as hauling the automatic vacuum-operated swimming-pool cleaner out of the pool to see why it had suddenly stopped working.

Please consult pages 15 to 25 of your operating manual for further information, unless you have already thrown your operating manual into the pool.

*2. DINING-ROOM FURNITURE MADE OUT OF RAILWAY SLEEPERS.* Before the invention of dining-room furniture made out of railway sleepers in Phalaborwa in 1968, few people even gave a second thought to the possibility that there might be another use for railway sleepers aside from being slept on by railways.

One person who did give the issue a second thought was

*An early step in the process of manufacturing dining-room furniture from railway sleepers.*

Frikkie de Witt, a qualified manufacturer of railway sleepers working under contract to the South African Railways.

While manufacturing a sleeper one day, a practice technically referred to as 'sleeping', Frikkie decided that he needed a larger surface to work on, so he asked his 14 assistants to please place the sleeper on top of his dining-room table.

Unfortunately, shortly after this was done, the dining-room table collapsed under the weight of the railway sleeper. That night, having fired his 14 assistants for sleeping on the job, Frikkie de Witt was forced to eat his evening meal of frikkadels and wood chips while seated on a railway sleeper around a railway sleeper.

It was at this point that Frikkie had his second thought. 'Hmmm,' he thought, 'I wonder what time Morkels are open tomorrow, and if they're having a sale on cast-iron dining-room tables.'

If you would like to manufacture your own dining-room furniture from railway sleepers, please note that it is illegal to remove sleepers from railway lines unless you are equipped with a very large crowbar.

*3. THE TWIST-OFF BEER-BOTTLE TOP.* Before the invention of the twist-off beer-bottle top in Nigel in 1969, people who wanted to enjoy a bottle of beer were often forced to prise the bottle open by clamping it tightly between the jaws of the person who forgot to bring the bottle-opener.

It was one such person, a qualified fitter-and-turner named Frikkie de Beer, who came up with the simple yet revolutionary idea of inventing a twist-off beer-bottle top while having his false teeth repaired after an HNP picnic in the picturesque East Rand mining-town of Nigel.

As it turned out, and also as it twisted off, the twist-off beer-bottle top proved to be an enormous success, and Frikkie sold the patent to a South African brewery for R250 000. Unfortunately, at the next HNP picnic in Nigel, Frikkie forgot to bring the beers.

*4. THE PLASTIC TWO-LITRE COOL-DRINK BOTTLE FILLED WITH WATER AND LEFT ON THE LAWN TO KEEP THE DOG OFF.* Before the invention of the plastic two-litre cool-drink bottle filled with water and left on the lawn to keep the dog off, suburban residents who wanted to keep dogs off their lawn were forced to resort to methods that have been described as 'cruel and unusual' by the United Nations Commission on Canine Rights.

In a report filed by a watchdog monitoring organisation based in Brakpan, these methods were found to include: running out of the house and shouting 'Voetsak!' at the dog; fencing lawn with low-voltage electric perimeter wire designed to give a mild shock to anyone who tripped over it while chasing dogs off the lawn; playing Bles Bridges records at frequencies only dogs can hear; and pelting dogs with empty plastic two-litre cool-drink bottles.

The organisation even monitored one incident in which a householder hurled a plastic two-litre cool-drink bottle filled with water at a Maltese Poodle that had allegedly been loitering with intent in the vicinity of a prize khakibos.

'I find that the empty plastic two-litre cool-drink bottles do not have enough velocity to sufficiently deter the alleged canine,' explained Mr Rex Gardener of Pampoenpoort.

Although the bottle missed the Maltese Poodle and ricocheted off the khakibos to land in the middle of the lawn, Mr Gardener has not been bothered by dogs of any variety since.

Scientists, dog-experts, and manufacturers of plastic cool-drink bottles have been unable to explain why a plastic two-litre cool-drink bottle filled with water should be so effective in keeping a dog off a lawn. But there can be no doubt that the system works.

Just ask any suburban householder with a lawn full of unsightly yellow patches shaped like plastic two-litre cool-drink bottles.

*5. THE PRE-CAST CONCRETE SECURITY WALL THAT IS SUPPOSED TO LOOK AS IF IT IS MADE OUT OF BRICKS.* What looks like a real brick wall, feels like a real brick wall, lasts like a real brick wall, and protects your home and property like a real brick wall? The answer, of course, is 'a real brick wall', but if you can't afford one, don't worry.

Thanks to a major technological breakthrough in the field of generic brick simulation in South Africa, it is now possible to enclose your property with a pre-cast concrete wall designed to look exactly like a brick wall under certain lighting conditions, such as a power failure in the middle of the night.

These simulated walls are so amazingly realistic, that they are often mistaken for the real thing by people who have never even seen a brick wall. Modelled from actual photographs of real brick walls, and painstakingly hand-painted by some of South Africa's top forgers of R50 notes, the pre-cast concrete wall that is supposed to look as if it is made out of bricks is the ideal solution for all householders who would like to keep their real brick walls safely hidden from public view.

*The water-filled plastic cool-drink bottle canine-deterrent device...
one of South Africa's Top Ten inventions.*

*6. THE BUMPER-STICKER THAT LOOKS LIKE A SPLAT OF PAINT.* Before the invention of the bumper-sticker that looks like a splat of paint in Bloemfontein in 1991, any person who spilled paint on some bloke's brand-new metallic-green Mazda would have had a lot of covering-up to do.

'I'm really sorry, I was just walking down the street reading the instructions on this can of yellow paint when I very foolishly attempted to cross at the green traffic light as you came roaring through the orange traffic light at 120 kilometres per hour, which you are fully entitled to do on account of the fact that you own the road. Please accept my sincere apologies, and allow me to remove this splat of paint with my tongue.'

Now such everyday incidents can be a thing of the past, thanks to the easy availability of reasonable facsimiles of paint splats in a variety of sizes, colours, and splats.

Simply peel off the complimentary adhesive backing, position carefully over splat of paint, and apply to surface of vehicle using side of fist. Smooth out any small air-bubbles with rolling-pin, and touch-up minor blemishes or colour deviations with easy-to-use 'Paint Splat' paint.

Coming soon: the bumper-sticker that looks like a bumper-sticker someone tried to chisel off his car before realising it was only a bumper-sticker.

*7. THE BALLPOINT PEN MANUFACTURED FROM A RECYCLED SEMI-AUTOMATIC RIFLE BULLET.* Whether you want to shoot off a quick letter of complaint to the building sub-contractor who put in your bathroom, sign your name with a flourish at the bottom of a Riot Insurance claim form, or send someone an internal memorandum saying 'You're Fired', you can't go wrong with a ballpoint pen manufactured from a recycled semi-automatic rifle bullet.

Meticulously hand-crafted from genuine Army Surplus cartridge cases, these titanium-tipped writing instruments are guaranteed to give your official correspondence that extra stamp of conviction.

Simply press down on the top of the ballpoint pen manufactured from a recycled semi-automatic rifle bullet, and a jet-inked roller-ball will shoot out for blot-free joined-up writing of the finest calibre. If this does not happen, please check to make sure that you have not loaded your writing instrument into your semi-automatic rifle by mistake.

Recommended by the Writing Desk of the Pan Africanist Congress for replying to all invitations to participate in the National Peace Accord, the ballpoint pen manufactured from a recycled semi-automatic rifle bullet is available in packs of 100 from your nearest stationery supplier.

Don't forget to pick up a couple of magazines on the way out.

*8. THE UNDERWATER SHARK-NET SHARK-ATTACK BARRIER.* Painstakingly crocheted from hundreds of thousands of adjustable shark-net bracelets, the underwater shark-net shark-attack barrier has proved to be one of the most effective methods of preventing shark attacks since the last sequel to *Jaws*.

In fact, not one shark is reported to have been attacked in South African waters since the measure was introduced off the Natal coast in 1962. Successfully field-tested on Great White Sharks, Not-So-Great White Sharks, Hammerhead Sharks, Who-You-Calling-A-Hammerhead Sharks, Ragged-Tooth Sharks, Shark-Toothed Sharks, Sand

Sharks, Second-Hand Car Salesmen and Transvalers Wearing Strap-On Plastic Shark Fins, this simple yet revolutionary measure can also be used to mark the far-side goal for your next game of underwater hockey.

But watch out for the sharks.

*9. THE EXPANDABLE CARDBOARD INNER-WINDSCREEN WITH SUNGLASSES ON THE OUTSIDE.* As the merciless South African sun beats down on cars in shopping-centre parking-lots, serious damage can be caused to the sensitive and finely-spun fibres of the fur on your dashboard.

Many motorists have returned from their daily shopping expeditions to discover that the sun's relentless ultra-violet rays have drained all the lime-green colouring from their dashboard fur, leaving it looking as listless and faded as a person who has spent half the day shopping and the other half trying to find his car.

The answer to at least part of this problem is to install an expandable cardboard inner-windscreen behind your windscreen before you step out of your car.

The tough, 'sun-resistant' outer layer of the cardboard will deflect even the most ferocious solar heatwaves, while the patented corrugated insulation acts as a powerful barrier between the outer layer of cardboard and the inner layer of cardboard.

On top of that, an attractive portrait of a pair of sunglasses is thrown in to facilitate identification of your vehicle in an open parking-lot. You may also choose from a variety of other designs, including cartoon characters, girls in bikinis, and advertising slogans for expandable cardboard inner-windscreens.

Please note that it is illegal to drive a vehicle with an

*Sneeze wire ... the acceptable face of riot control in South Africa today.*

expandable cardboard inner-windscreen still in place, unless you are trying to avoid being recognised by your creditors.

*10. THE INSTANT RAZOR-WIRE BARRICADE WITH SNEEZING-POWDER ON TOP.* The instant razor-wire barricade (just add protesters) was invented by the Mass Action Demotivation Unit of the South African Police as an easy-to-install obstacle to constitutional negotiations.

By pulling a lever inside a specially customised armoured vehicle, a policeman wearing a specially customised suit of armour is able to unleash gleaming coils of razor-embedded stainless-steel designed to give the forces of law and order a cutting edge in any conflict situation.

Unfortunately, no one has yet figured out how to get the razor-wire back into the armoured vehicle once the protesters have gone home. As a result, thousands of metres of valuable razor-wire coils have been liberated for use as shrub-protectors, twin-blade razor-refills, mouse-traps, salad-slicers, and instant razor-wire barricades against the police.

In order to cut down on this practice, the Razor-Wire Theft Squad of the Mass Action Demotivation Unit came up with the ingenious idea of sprinkling liberal quantities of sneezing-powder over the razor-wire before it is dispatched for use.

Based on the scientifically proven theory that a person is less likely to liberate or attempt to surmount an instant razor-wire barricade if he has a sneezing fit while doing so, the instant razor-wire barricade with sneezing-powder on top has become one of the biggest success stories in the history of South African riot control. Gezundheit.

# *How To Become A Top Rugby Player And Beat The All-Blacks With One Foot Tied Behind Your Back*

According to *Laws of the Game of Rugby Football*, a thin book available from the fiction section of any reputable bookstore, rugby football is a game played between two teams of 15 players each, or one team of 15 players and two lock forwards who have been taking something to get rid of their cough.

Rugby football is a fast-moving, hard-hitting, pile-driving sport, played by men of exceptional substance under the most trying conditions.

In a recent investigation by the Exceptional Substances Squad of the South African Rugby Football Police, these substances were found to include: one packet of fast-acting, extra-strength headache tablets for instant relief from being hit on the head by one packet of fast-acting, extra-strength naartjies; 500 grams of pure, uncut 'grass', found under prop forward's tongue after sliding tackle near base of goalpost; one hand-held 'Minty Breath' aerosol spray for aiming at members of opposing team during a scrummage; one tube of quick-drying 'Superglue' for repairing split boot-heels and replacing dentures; one large tub of 'Ball Gleam' polish for polishing leather rugby ball at half-time; two extra-large cough-lozenges for sticking in ear-drums whenever referee blows whistle to indicate foul; one big jar of 'Wintergreen' liniment for smearing on aching joints and muscles because it smells nice.

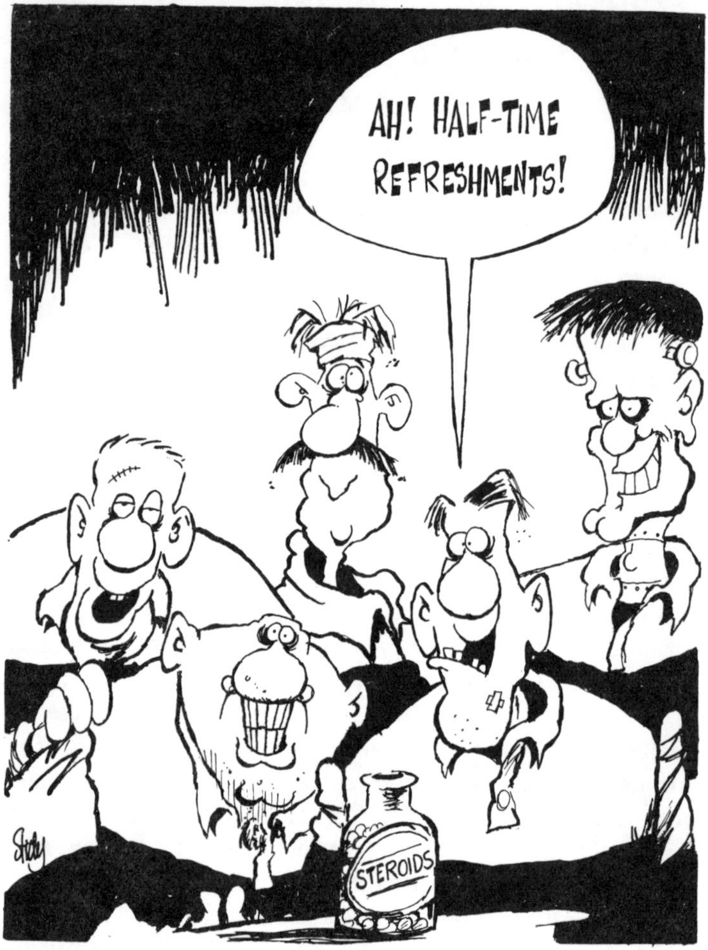
AH! HALF-TIME REFRESHMENTS!
STEROIDS

Despite this haul, described by official sources as 'one of the longest paragraphs we've ever come across', the Exceptional Substances Squad of the South African Rugby Football Police still managed to lose the match by 220 points to six, the six being scored while the other team were still in their dressing-room snorting 'Deep Heat' at the start of the second half.

As a result of this incident, the Fair Play and Amateur Code Preservation Committee of the South African Rugby Football Union (Retired) has decided to institute strict 'anti-dope' measures before and after every rugby football match played under its auspices.

From now on, no rugby football player will be allowed to participate in any club, league, provincial, international, or interdenominational competition without first being tested for possession of any item other than the ball. Even then, the ball will be subject to inspection by an authorised German Shepherd.

'We are determined to go out of our way to throw the book at any rugby football players who are found to be in contravention of sub-section six (i) of paragraph 2 (a) of section 64 (brackets) of the Transvaal Provincial Road Traffic Regulations and Amendments,' said a spokesman, adding that it was difficult to throw a book as thin as *Laws of the Game of Rugby Football*.

The spokesman added that the 'anti-dope' test would be conducted on an individual basis in a specially constructed cubicle, and that the questions would be multiple-choice. Here are some examples:

1. Are you now, or have you ever been, in possession of any illegal and/or prohibited substances specifically designed or intended to enhance your stamina, physique, speed,

muscle-to-weight ratio, and chances of tackling Naas Botha?

a) Yes, but I never inhaled.

b) No, but I'll see what I can organise for you after the match.

c) Er, I am Naas Botha.

2. Have you stopped using anabolic steroids yet?

a) Yes, I'm absolutely positive.

b) No, I still feel a little bit fluey.

c) Excuse me, what do you think you're doing with that bottle?

3. What is your position on the use of illegal and/or prohibited substances by rugby football players?

a) Lock forward.

b) Right wing.

c) Sitting on the bench, eating naartjies.

Any player who fails to score at least 50 per cent in these tests will immediately be suspended from taking part in further tests for the duration of the season. Further penalties will be considered if the aforesaid player fails to score a set number of further penalties in matches played during this time.

These measures may seem harsh, but they are vital if the reputation of South African rugby is to be preserved for future generations.

'We will take whatever action is necessary to ensure that fair play, gentlemanly conduct, and the integrity of the amateur code are upheld as fundamental elements of the traditional game of all-in jukskei,' vowed a spokesman for the All-In Jukskei Board of South Africa.

'Er, I was wondering if you'd mind participating in a simple scientific test . . . on second thoughts, maybe we can wait until after the match.'

A spokesman for the South African Rugby Football Union said he was unable to comment at the moment, as he was busy negotiating film, television, merchandising and 087 rights for the forthcoming tour of South Africa by the British Lions, the Tasmanian Devils, the French Frogs, the Argentinian Pumas, the Samoan Tigers, and the Welsh Daffodils.

If you are interested in attending any of these historic international test-matches, please note that no person will be allowed into the stadium while under the influence of any prohibited substance, unless he has come to play rugby.

## *Will The Last Person To Leave The Country Please Turn Off The Light At The End Of The Tunnel*
### *(A practical guide for outwardly-mobile ex-patriots)*

As South Africa moves closer and closer towards a genuine democracy, more and more South Africans are getting the urge to move closer and closer towards a genuine democracy, such as England, Australia, New Zealand, Canada, Belgium, Russia, the United States, and anywhere else that has a vacancy.

While outwardly-mobile South Africans may once have been accused of selfishness and a lack of the pioneering spirit that made this country what it is today, they are now free to leave with a clear conscience, having played their role in setting South Africa on the high road to peace and democracy.

To get on the high road to peace and democracy, take the turnoff that says 'Jan Smuts Airport', and follow the arrows to the International Departures Lounge.

Please hand your passport and one-way air ticket to the United Nations peacekeeping soldier on duty, and you will be allowed to board your plane as soon as some of the bigger barricades have been removed from the runway.

You are reminded that delays of up to several hours could be experienced, depending on the number of people attempting to cling to the wings and fuselage of your jetliner once the doors have been closed.

If you have been lucky enough to get a seat, make sure that your seatbelt is securely fastened, your hand-luggage is stowed, and the knees of the person behind you have pushed the back of your seat into an upright position.

In terms of international emigration regulations, an air-hostess will now walk down the aisle with a can of disinfectant in her hand. If you are concerned that you may be allergic to the spray of fine mist, now is the time to get out a handkerchief, cover your nose and mouth, and bid a misty-eyed farewell to the land of your birth.

But before you do, there are a couple of small procedures and formalities to get out of the way. Thank you, and have a nice relocation.

## *Where to go from here, and how to get there*

Leaving the country of one's birth for a new home in a strange and faraway land is never an easy thing to do. As any settler will tell you, it is a process fraught with anguish, emotional turmoil, agonising indecision and prolonged soul-searching.

Many formerly contented South African families have been torn apart by furious arguments over whether it is better to go to Toronto and put up with the weather, Los Angeles and put up with the earthquakes, or Sydney and put up with the Australians.

In order to avoid this kind of conflict, it is recommended that you use the following proven method of 'Random Resettlement Location Selection', preferably before you book your outward flight.

To begin with, you will need a large, full-colour map of the world, obtainable from any major airline office when the lady behind the counter isn't looking.

You will also need a pair of 'dividers', which you will find lying next to the protractor in your maths set.

If you can't find your protractor, any two-pronged metallic instrument will do.

Now spread the map out in front of you, carefully smoothing out any folds, creases, or mountain ranges, and open the dividers so that one point is pointing up, and the other is pointing down.

You are now ready to make one of the most vital decisions of your life. Shut your eyes tightly, wave the dividers in the air for a bit, and jab the downward point into the map with a firm, decisive action. We will now take a short break while you remove the dividers from your thigh, and then we can try again with the map spread out on the dining-room table.

Remember that the aim of the exercise is to determine, by objective and empirical means, the country to whose embassy you and your family should apply for permanent residence or refugee status. To make the process as fair as possible, the map should be spun around on its axis a few times, and no correspondence should be entered into once the dividers have made their mark.

It is only after having carefully and unanimously decided that you do not really want to emigrate to Beirut, Albania, the North Pole, the middle of the Atlantic Ocean, the Bermuda Triangle, the pot-plant on your dining-room table, or South Africa, that you may go ahead and apply to the embassies of the following nations, which are always happy to accept South Africans under certain conditions.

## *A brief guide to some of the countries that are always happy to accept South Africans under certain conditions*

The following countries have indicated that they are willing to consider applications from South African citizens who are committed to peace, democracy, and the free movement of foreign currency.

Applications may be made in person at the Aspirant Emigrants Desk of the relevant consulates or embassies, most of which are open for business between 11 am and 11.02 am on any day of the week that does not fall on a weekday.

You will need at least two dozen passport photograph-sized passport-photographs of yourself or reasonable facsimile, and you will be asked to fill in some forms. Handwriting will be taken into account, so don't bother typing.

Since the emigration process can take several months, you are advised not to telephone or otherwise contact the embassy to find out how your application is coming along. When it is ready, they will open the window and give you a shout.

## THE UNITED STATES OF AMERICA

Since its founding by a bunch of emigrants more than 200 years ago, the United States of America has been a safe haven for people fleeing injustice, discrimination, and oppression in their own country.

If you can prove that your application for an American emigration visa was turned down purely on the grounds that you are a South African citizen, you may therefore have a case for reapplying as a victim of discrimination and injustice.

However, entry requirements are very strict, and you will have to satisfy a full board of US Immigration Authorities that you are capable of spelling words like 'potatoe', 'naturalization', and the name of the American Vice-President, Mr Dan Quail.

You will also be required to demonstrate competence in the following areas: chewing bubblegum and talking through nostrils; packing own groceries in big brown-paper bag without handles; filling own car with unleaded gas; driving the wrong way down a one-way street at 120 miles per hours in a Cadillac stretch limousine with sparks coming off the rear fender.

Should your application be refused, you have the right to appeal to the Mexican Embassy for a tourist visa with enclosed map showing best spots to swim across Rio Grande river and sneak under fence into Texas at midnight.

You will then be classified as an 'illegal alien', and you will not be allowed to do any work aside from brief non-speaking roles in the sequel to *Aliens 4*.

Many people are under the impression that you need a 'Green Card' in order to settle down and enjoy a comfortable lifestyle in the United States of America.

In fact, all you really need is a Gold Card. Thank you, and have a nice stay.

*Expatriate South African driver acclimatising to American road traffic system.*

## AUSTRALIA

Bluegum trees, rugged coastlines, sandy beaches, amazing animals, mysterious tribal cultures, friendly natives, and the best weather in the world. Yes, there's no doubt that South Africa is one of the most spectacular countries anyone could ever hope to visit for a couple of days.

But Australia, the world's biggest island and smallest continent, also has its points. One of these is the 'Australian Immigration Points System', according to which prospective immigrants are rated on their suitability for becoming Australians.

It is felt that this system provides the most objective and equitable method of ensuring that only the most acceptable candidates are accepted, and that no personal or political prejudice is allowed to stand in the way of the expatriate South African immigration official who adds up the score.

Points are awarded according to the following strict criteria, and no correspondence will be entered into as long as the Australian Postal Service is on strike.

* Can speak good English: *10 points.*
* Can speak fair dinkum Australian: *20 points.*
* Have internationally-recognised degree in Accounting, Dentistry, Civil Engineering, or similar profession: *15 points.*
* Can surf: *25 points.*
* Can bowl, bat, dive, and run better than any member of 1992 Australia World Cup cricket team: *5 points.*
* Think Australia should pull out of Commonwealth: *20 points.*
* Didn't know Australia was in Commonwealth: *40 points.*
* Can't stand Paul Keating: *50 points.*
* Don't know who Paul Keating is, but still can't stand

him: *52 points.*
* Know any good jokes about New Zealanders: *100 points.*

Along with your completed application form, you will be required to send three photographs of yourself in right, left, and centre profile, as well as a signed character reference from your parole officer.

*NEW ZEALAND*

New Zealand, so-called to avoid confusion with some other place called 'Zealand', is the small bit of New Zealand-shaped land to the right of Australia.

Actually, if you look at the map, there appear to be three bits of New Zealand-shaped land, plus a few scattered dots with 'NZ' in brackets after their name.

Contrary to popular belief, New Zealand is not a dull and dormant destination.

In fact, more than half of the country's 15 000 volcanoes are still classified as 'active'. If you would like to emigrate to New Zealand, you may apply in person at New Zealand, and if there is anybody home, they will be happy to provide you with the necessary application forms.

Persons who have qualifications and experience in the following fields are especially welcome: sheep-shearers; sheep-breeders; sheep-clippers; sheep-dippers; sheep-knitters; sheep-counters; sheep-dogs; shepherds; sheep-dogs named Shep; chartered accountants; and any other field with a bunch of sheep and a couple of New Zealanders in it.

*ENGLAND*

England, not to be confused with Great Britain or the United Kingdom, is a very popular emigration destination for people from former colonies of the British Empire.

If you were born before South Africa declared its independence from the Commonwealth in 1961, you are therefore automatically entitled to fill in a form and stand at the back of the queue. Filling in a form and standing at the back of the queue is one of the basic requirements for British citizenship, as is complaining about the weather while filling in a form and standing at the back of the queue.

Although the Home Office will do its best to accommodate all reasonable applications for British citizenship, you are reminded that the country is currently in the grip of a recession that has left thousands of people unemployed, such as Prince Edward.

Also, the roads are only wide enough for one elderly lady driver at a time, the motorways are clogged up with orange hatty things and men not at work, the beer is warm, the food is cold, the Prime Minister is boring, and it's always raining except when it's drizzling.

Other than that, you're welcome.

*RUSSIA*
As part of its continuing policy of social and political reform, the independent democratic republic of Russia is happy to accept applications for permanent residence from any South African who is not a communist. It would also be helpful if you were not too much of a capitalist, as there is not yet enough capital to go round.

Nevertheless, democratic socialists of all political persuasions will feel at home in this historic country as it shrugs off the yoke of authoritarian rule and strides boldly into a new era of new errors.

As yet, there is no Russian embassy in South Africa, but if you would like further information on how to become a citizen, feel free to ask the first Russian immigrant you bump into in Hillbrow.

## *CANADA*
Thanks to the recent disintegration of the Union of Soviet Socialist Republics, Canada today holds the official title of 'Largest Country in the World', although it is still only third on the 'Most Boring' list, after New Zealand and Belgium.

In any case, Canada's land-mass is so vast, that every man, woman, child, and Rottweiler currently residing in South Africa could fit inside its borders three-and-a-half times, as long as they promise to go back home immediately afterwards.

Because most of Canada consists of snow, however, the Canadian Government has unfortunately been forced to impose severe restrictions on population density, and South Africans will therefore only be accepted for permanent residence if they have an IQ of 160 or higher.

## *SOUTH AMERICA*
Contrary to popular belief and Americans who keep confusing it with South Africa, South America is not one big country, but is rather one big continent consisting of several countries.

Among these are Argentina, Brazil, Peru, Colombia, Uruguay (not to be confused with Paraguay), Paraguay (not to be confused with Uruguay), Chile, the Falkland Islands, and South America. Many of these countries are happy to accept South Africans who were only following orders and have nothing to hide beneath their fake moustaches, Panama hats, and chrome sunglasses.

With its golden, sun-drenched beaches, towering, snow-capped mountains, steamy, primeval rain-forests, and see-through ozone layer for easy all-over tanning, South America is the place to go for the patriotic South African who would like a change from corrupt dictatorships, bankrupt economies, States of Emergency, Banana Republics, and simmering social and political unrest.

Hey, at least you won't ever feel homesick.

## *What you may take with you, and how to get it out*

OK. You've settled on your new homeland, you've been awarded your emigration visas, you've booked your discount one-way tickets, you've resigned from your job, you've cancelled the milk deliveries, you've cashed in your unit trusts, you've retired your domestic servant, you've put your house on the market.

Now comes the difficult bit. Packing. Hang on a second. Maybe you shouldn't retire your domestic servant just yet.

This is a job that is going to require all the assistance, advice, and additional muscle power your domestic servant can get, so put your feet up, order something to drink, and follow the following guidelines for a stress-free packing experience.

To begin with, you should be aware that the South African Government has imposed certain restrictions and limitations on the effects you may take with you to your new destination, unless you are only going as far as Bophuthatswana.

In all other cases, the following quotas must be strictly observed, or else you will not be allowed to leave the country. Please note that these quotas do not apply if you are a member of the present Government.

*'... but I thought you said you packed the tickets!'*

*Money:* You may take a maximum of R200 000 per household, plus all the Dollars, Yen, Deutschmark, Sterling, Swiss Franc, Pula, Escudos, and Roubles you can fit in your underwear.

*Household Goods:* You may take any large household item of value that hasn't already been stolen for insurance purposes. Please note that any item larger than a medium-sized facsimile machine, or reasonable facsimile thereof, will have to go by boat, while any item larger than a boat will have to go by ship.

*Krugerrands:* You may take all the Krugerrands you can carry in your hand-luggage, providing they are made of chocolate. You don't want to bother with the gold ones. They're not valuable enough.

*Motor Vehicles:* You may take one motor vehicle per household, unless you can get somebody else to give you a lift to the airport. This is a good idea, as you will save a lot on parking fees when you come back to South Africa two years later to look for a job.

*Pets:* You may take a maximum of two cats and two dogs per household, providing they are able to pay for their own tickets. Please note that because of the very strict quarantine procedures applied in most foreign countries, your animals will have to spend up to six months locked in cages at the airport quarantine station. Accommodation for owners is available at a nominal rate.

*Foodstuffs:* You do not really need to take any foodstuffs with you, as there will be something to eat on the plane. If you are not hungry, however, you may take a maximum of 200 000 calories worth of light snacks of South African origin in your hand-luggage. This should amount to one medium-sized vetkoek, or two low-cal koeksisters without syrup.

*Warning:* Biltong, droëwors, frikkadels, or any similar delicacy may not be exported under any conditions, in order to protect caterers supplying the South African expatriate market overseas.

*Cultural Weapons:* There is no restriction on the amount of cultural weapons you may take overseas with you. In fact, it would be very nice if you could take the lot.

Once you have sorted out the items you would like to take with you from the items you would like to donate to your domestic servant, it's time to move on to the next big step. Calling in the movers.

Look under 'Movers' in the Yellow Pages, and telephone their offices in alphabetical order. In each case, the number should be answered by a constant engaged signal. If it is not, and you actually hear a telephone ring, do not be alarmed. It will simply mean that the movers have left the country.

In the meantime, you may want to ask your domestic servant if she would mind organising your belongings into the following convenient pre-packing categories.

*Not Fragile:* any items unlikely to be damaged in transit, such as cast-iron potjiekos pots, stainless-steel wine-fermentation vats, rubber mallets, and dining-room furniture manufactured from railway sleepers.

*Fragile:* any items likely to be damaged in transit, such as crystal chandeliers, long-playing records, window-panes, fine China tea-sets, bottles of vintage wine, and packing-crates marked 'Fragile, Please Handle With Care'.

*Extremely Fragile:* any items already damaged in transit, such as confidential emigration documents opened in error by the Post Office, antique Chippendale sofas stuffed with Krugerrands, and framed copies of the National Peace Accord.

All items in the last two categories should be carefully wrapped in tissue-paper, cheesecloth, Sunday newspaper supplements, extraordinary editions of the *Government Gazette,* and two double-layers of bubble-wrap.

On second thoughts, keep the bubble-wrap. Hold between thumb and forefinger, and press down tightly until you hear a popping sound. Move on to next bubble, and repeat.

This is a very effective method of relieving stress and tension while you wait for the movers to come around and inform you that you have made it on to the secondary sub-waiting-list, and that someone will be coming around to give you a quote one of these days.

In the meantime, you may want to begin drafting that all-important 'Relocation Confirmation Note', for sending to friends, family, business acquaintances, and the Receiver of Revenue.

*What to say in your relocation confirmation note to friends, family, business acquaintances, and people you owe lots of money*

According to the rules of emigration etiquette, it is not considered good form to leave the country without filling in one of those little blue forms at the airport, where you will finally be able to write 'Leaving the country' in the space reserved for REASON FOR TRAVEL/DOEL VAN REIS.

Before you do, however, you may want to pop a few photostated copies of your Relocation Confirmation Note in the postbox alongside the souvenir shop in the Departure Lounge.

Commemorative envelopes and stamps are available from the souvenir shop. Well, what else are you going to do with the South African coins in your pocket?

## RELOCATION CONFIRMATION NOTE

TO: Friends, family, business acquaintances, creditors, former employers, and anyone still waiting for the movers to come around

RE: Relocation

Hi!

This is just a short note to confirm that we are leaving the country with immediate effect and all the Financial Rands we can fit in our hand-luggage.

That is to say, all the Financial Rands we are legally entitled to fit in our hand-luggage in terms of the Foreign Exchange Control Regulations Act of 1974, plus Amendments.

You may want to know what has made us decide to leave the land of our birth at this point in its history. Well, the major motivating factor has definitely been the Foreign Exchange Control Regulations Act of 1974, plus Amendments.

But aside from that, our unilateral decision was also prompted by the following considerations, in conjunction with a thorough and objective analysis of the available options:

1. Despite our most fervent hopes and dreams, we do not foresee any possibility of a long-term improvement in the quality of South African television.

2. Notwithstanding the fact that we voted 'Yes', South Africa still only finished fourth in the World Cup cricketing contest.

3. We can't stand cricket, anyway.

4. On the advice of our broker, we invested a considerable sum of money in shares, stocks, bonds, gilts, debentures, unit trusts and futures on the Johannesburg Stock Exchange. Unfortunately, our broker moved to Toronto the following day, and we still haven't been able to find out what a 'debenture' is supposed to be.

5. We can no longer afford the increased monthly premiums on our Civil War insurance.

6. We weren't even able to get Negotiated Settlement & Non-Racial Democratic Elections insurance.

7. Our emigration visas finally arrived!

8. So did the movers.

9. Hey, did you know that you can get up to 50 per cent off your one-way air-ticket if you show your emigration visa when you book through the national airline of the country to which you are emigrating?

Of course, it goes without saying that we will miss South Africa with all our hearts and minds, and that we will be first in the queue to come back home as soon as the transition to a peaceful and democratic society has run its course.

But before we go without saying that, we would like to issue the following simple yet heartfelt declaration to whom it may concern:

TO WHOM IT MAY CONCERN
We, the undersigned, do hereby declare that we are leaving the country, hereinafter referred to as 'South Africa', and that we are not to be held responsible for any outstanding

debts that may have been incurred by us before we decided to leave the country.

On the other hand, should any cheques, postal orders, loan levy repayments, or sweepstakes notification certificates arrive for us at our old address, kindly forward by registered post to the forwarding address indicated on the outside of the envelope.

Don't worry about the Army call-up papers or the voter registration cards.

OK, Bye,

The Undersigned

PS: It goes without saying that you're more than welcome to pop in and say hello if you're ever in the neighbourhood. It would also be nice if you could bring along one or more of the following items:

1. Up-to-date property supplement for the Johannesburg metropolitan area.
2. Up-to-date 'Situations Vacant' section of classified advertising supplement.
3. One-way air-ticket back to South Africa.

Just in case. Thanks.